KITEZH:
A community approach to
raising children in Russia

KITEZH

A community approach to
raising children in Russia

DIMITRY MOROZOV

First published in Great Britain by Eland Publishing Limited,
61 Exmouth Market, London EC1R 1XR in June 2008,
with the assistance of a grant from the Big Lottery Fund

Supported by

ISBN 978 1 906011 36 9

Text set by Nick Randall
Printed in Navarra, Spain by GraphyCems

Contents

Acknowledgments

We would like to express our gratitude to Kitezh volunteers Ruth Ahmedzai and Laura Casiraghi for translating the original draft of the book, and to Emily Justice for her translation of extracts. Many other volunteers have contributed to this book as editors and translators. Special thanks for careful editing to David Baggett-Fyten and Joseph Kilpatrick of the Centre for Purposeful Living, North Carolina, USA and to Andrew Aikman, Bill Cobb, Liza Hollingshead and Rhiannon Hanfman. We also acknowledge the Big Lottery Fund in the United Kingdom for providing the funding to make this publication possible, and Rose Baring at Eland for publishing it.

Preface

Kitezh: a community approach to raising children in Russia is written by the founder of the Kitezh community, Dimitry Morozov. It is the distillation of his unique experience of fifteen years spent developing this community. The academic and scientific ideas elaborated here have grown from the writer's experience. In the book he looks at the stages of childhood development and the psychological idiosyncrasies of children who have lost their parents. In an easy-to-read style, the author explains how to create a safe environment for children, and how to bring together the strengths of those enthusiastic about creating a therapeutic community harmoniously. Especially valuable is the fact that what he writes is founded on his practical experience. The natural way of life in the community provides an answer to the toughest questions of bringing up children.

I call the thoughts and experience of Dimitry Morozov 'humane pedagogy', based on trial and error and life-learned wisdom. It will be easier to understand and to accept the ideas and experience of this self-taught educator if we imagine the environment in which they have arisen—traditional Russian surroundings, with their national psychological idiosyncrasies. In difficult social and economical conditions this group of good and spiritually inclined people is trying to build a new way of life based on prioritising the work with children.

I have opened my eyes to certain realities of Kitezh practice, which perhaps do not quite conform to the generally accepted framework of child-rearing, but I gladly welcome the surprising search led by these people, which demonstrates determination to give themselves totally to the children. I think that this book will call many to join the service of disadvantaged children. Dimitry Morozov will sound the bell of conscience in the souls of many Russians.

Shalva Amonashvili
Academic of the Russian Academy of Education
Doctor of Psychology
Director of the Laboratory of Humane Pedagogy
at Moscow State University

Introduction

It is particularly rare these days to find leaders of educational or social initiatives writing about their work while they are actually doing it. Somehow the exacting task of sustaining hands-on work day in, day out, with young people and those who teach and care for them precludes any time for putting down on paper exactly what is happening. By defying this trend Dimitry Morozov joins the small band of practitioner-authors that exist, in the field of working with disturbed and damaged children in need of a therapeutic solution to their difficulties.

Kitezh deserves to be written about. In its fifteen years of existence several enthusiastic reports have appeared both in the foreign press and in Russia. Like the mystical city in the old Russian legend after which it is named, Kitezh Children's Community does indeed symbolise the potential dawn of a new age in addressing the needs of Russia's orphan children, and there are now the first welcome signs that those responsible for shaping national policy may be taking an active interest.

What is the special nature of the approach practised by Morozov and those who have come to join him at Kitezh? It is, firstly, the deinstitutionalising of childcare. Kitezh does not warehouse children for the convenience of the authorities. It is a truly child-centred village of supported foster families where a rigorous education programme, together with a group and individual therapeutic process designed to empower the most disempowered of children, flourishes. Where the children feel that, at last, they have reached a place where they are safe, valued and where life, with all its burdens, can also embrace the freedom to play and have fun.

At Kitezh, the unlovable are loved and outrageous behaviour learned on the streets of Russia's towns and cities because there was no other option is tolerated, worked with and turned around. This may sound simplistic to some ears but that is what happens there with very few exceptions. The very process of empowerment to which I referred becomes the child's prime tool in marking his recovery as he learns to own the process of his own healing and growth. The foster family he has joined is not 'administered' from a distant social services office but supported and nourished on an hour by hour basis, year round, by others carrying out the same role for other children, and enhanced by the dynamic presence of their natural children whose contribution to the process cannot be overstated.

Here the novice foster parent is taught by the experience of those who have practised the art for several years. This, however, has never been enough for Kitezh. Morozov has actively sought the experience of social innovators and practitioners from abroad, invited them to Kitezh to observe freely, comment and suggest ways forward in the light of their extensive work with similarly dysfunctional children. Then, with a cool dispassionate professionalism and loyal to his first principles which he has laboured hard to determine, he and his colleagues have selectively transposed this wisdom into the Russian context and made it work for Kitezh.

Kitezh is now an international associate of the Charterhouse Group of therapeutic communities, UK, with a strong list of standards of care and education to look to for support. The Group conference of 2003, held in England, first read of, and then heard from Morozov and one other community from Denmark and proposed Kitezh be admitted to membership. This proposal was endorsed by the whole Charterhouse Group later the same year thereby setting up a process by which Kitezh adults can engage in useful exchanges of visits, current ideas and practice with some of the most successful organisations who have worked therapeutically over many years with troubled children. This is already happening.

Following several advisory missions over ten years to Russian ministries, regional authorities and individual children's houses and schools, it has been my joy and privilege over the last five years to witness and perhaps contribute to the development of this remarkable community. It has embarked on yet another big step: the foundation of a second village, Orion. This challenge will harness every skill the people at Kitezh have learned to date. The courage they have demonstrated in getting this far in a sometimes sceptical society will serve them well. They now have tangible support for their innovative work from within Russia and in time will, I very much hope, make some positive professional impact on thinking and practice throughout the whole country. This book will help in making the journey.

David Dean OBE

NOTE

In 1978 David Dean OBE founded Raddery School in Scotland, a therapeutic school for children with special needs where he worked with forty children and forty staff members for seventeen years, developing an innovative residential programme based on holistic and group psychotherapeutic principles. The school had an active small farm, outdoor education programme and a flourishing use of music and drama. The children's educational, social, emotional and spiritual development together with a strong involvement in community decision-making were outstanding features of Raddery.

Currently in semi-retirement, David acts, through the Ecologia Youth Trust, as an international advisor and consultant to Kitezh. In the same year that he was honoured with an OBE in the UK, the Ministry of Education in Moscow honoured him for assisting in their programme of change in special schools, orphanages and special vocational schools. He also contributes, as a visiting lecturer, to course work for students in the psychology and sociology departments at the State University of St Petersburg.

He lives with his wife Valery in Nethybridge in the Cairngorms National Park in Scotland where they welcome visitors from throughout the world to their Lazy Duck Hostel and two holiday cottages.

Introduction

This book is dedicated to parents, foster parents, adoptive parents and teachers. It is aimed at those who consider raising children to be one of life's highest callings and one of the highest forms of art. It describes the scientific and practical elements of a truly exceptional experiment: the formation and development of the first therapeutic community in Russia. The name of this therapeutic community is Kitezh.

We, the foster parents of the Kitezh community, view our endeavour as a 'community' because it is simultaneously an educational complex, a social experiment, a form of local administration, and a cooperative way of living. Kitezh celebrated its fifteenth anniversary in 2007. We have attained relative stability and are a home and source of inspiration for fifty adults and children. Our primary achievement in the first fifteen years is the fact that we still exist at all. We have been, and remain, an experiment.

Our second achievement, which sets Kitezh apart from prevalent theories and practices of child rearing worldwide, is our success at combining the inherent advantages of individual family structure with a communitarian or cooperative form of social organisation and child-raising.

WHAT IS UNIQUE ABOUT KITEZH'S STRUCTURE?

The basic unit of Kitezh is the foster family. In 2003 there were ten families. All of the families share a common financial source, legal protection, household management, and a united approach to education. Every adult fulfills a variety of responsibilities in schooling our children and maintaining the community while serving simultaneously as a foster parent. Adults with various technical and professional skills, working side by side with the children in doing the day-to-day tasks of the community, provides maximum efficiency in using our limited human and financial resources.

Our greatest challenge has been to combine in one holistic organisation the family, a school, a social structure and a non-government organisation that must be run in accordance with the laws of state organisations with whom we are obliged to cooperate. Our system is a form of synergy that combines love, trust and family warmth with the necessity to go to school and fulfill societal obligations. Within this complex milieu, the family, with all its psychological nuances, goes about its day-to-day life in accordance with its first priority of educating and developing children who were robbed of their biological parents and placed in harsh circumstances.

Legally, we are a non-commercial partnership of foster families, but we are not entirely sure this is the best choice of title, as the merging of such social constructs as the family, a public organisation, and a state institution remains an unfamiliar concept in Russia. The highest legislative body in Kitezh is the Council of Members of the Non-Commercial Partnership. The highest executive position is the Head of the Community, a post that is elected annually. The Teachers' Council, of which all foster parents and schoolteachers are automatically members, decides all issues related to the children's education and upbringing. The Financial Council manages communal financing and agriculture under the leadership of the Financial Director. In practice, it is the Teachers' Council that has the deciding word, as the children's upbringing is of prime importance in Kitezh.

THE SCIENTIFIC BASIS OF OUR WORK

We started to build our therapeutic community and take in children inspired by the idealistic concept that a child needs nothing more than love from his new parents and a normal environment with kind and intelligent people. True to Russian custom, we plunged in headlong, only later learning the practical aspects of raising children as we went along.

We came to realise that common sense and life experience alone were inadequate in working with children with developmental problems. It was necessary to seek a more reliable model for foster parenting. We were fortunate to discover appropriate theories and specialists who could show us a better approach to putting theory into practice. We have yet to discover, however, an all-encompassing theory to shield us from the multitude of problems we encounter. Within the community, we create our relationships, develop our educational framework and construct our houses based upon the priority of serving the children's developmental needs. The practicalities of raising children dictate our direction. We attempt, as the renowned Georgian teacher, Shalva Amonashvili stated, 'to develop and bring up a child with the help of life itself'.

We were fortunate to develop close and cooperative relationships with foreign professionals with whom we discovered much common ground in our respective approaches to therapy and child rearing. Psychologists and social workers from Great Britain provided valuable guidance for the training of our foster parents. Three of our mothers mastered the practice of non-directive play therapy, thanks to Barbara Smedley, Christine Taylor and Margery Bray. Bray's book *Poppies on a Rubbish Heap* brought our attention to latent problems such as sexual abuse of infants. Beverley A'Court introduced art therapy into our therapeutic work with children with excellent results. David Dean, the founder of Raddery, a unique school for troubled teenagers in Great Britain, helped us convert to a professional psychotherapeutic organisation. Among the measures we have implemented, thanks to David's guidance, are daily teachers' councils, community therapeutic meetings and play therapy sessions; and we have begun to keep a personal progress record for each child.

We extend a special thank you to the Scottish charity Ecologia Youth Trust and its director, Liza Hollingshead, as well as the British funds Charity Know How and the Big Lottery Fund, which financed our training programme with the British specialists.

WE, THE KITEZHANS

When the word 'orphan' is used we know that many immediately imagine a stray mini-gangster, dirty, aggressive, and ill bred. Sometimes our children come to Kitezh exactly like this. But once they arrive here, they cease being orphans. All of our children are intelligent, beautiful and diligent. They are not perfect, but they are just like children all over the world. They write poems and perform on stage, they practise martial arts and put out an Internet web site; they dance and study English. The greatest joy for us—the adults who work with and care for them—is knowing them, communicating with them and facilitating their growth.

We hope that by reading this book you too will experience this joy and become better acquainted with the art of bringing up a young personality and allowing the soul to shine.

1

Misha, Petya and the Minibus

The Gazelle minibus was made from metal by honest workmen. It was for this reason, no doubt, that it paused in contemplation for a few seconds after colliding with the birch tree before bursting into flames. This momentary time lapse gave Petya and Misha the chance to clamber out of it and run out of harm's way.

Someone driving by the scene informed Kitezh of what had happened, so three of us rushed to the scene of the accident, fire extinguisher at the ready but there was nothing to put out: all that remained of the Gazelle was charred remains. The boys had dashed off somewhere into the undergrowth, tormented by fear and guilt. One of us ran into the woods, tracked them down, and brought them back.

We paid a silent tribute to the remains of the faithful minibus, which had served us for five years on Russia's rural, potholed roads, and then returned to Kitezh. As we always do in extraordinary circumstances like this, we convened a general meeting of the community and the wrongdoers were called upon to answer numerous unpleasant questions. Misha and Petya honoured the community's values of honesty and sincerity and admitted what they had done, with an explanation of their motives as best they could.

The lads had been drinking vodka that night 'because it was a Saturday' and felt like going for a ride. Petya was an official driver for the community, so he opened the garage, backed out the minibus, and proceeded to amuse his brother. On impulse they decided to drive to Baryatino, the nearest village, where even at seven on a Sunday morning a person on the loose who knows the right people and places can get a drink. On the way, they conceived more daring ideas about visiting some pretty assistants who worked in the shop. If they had managed all that, who knows where they would have ended their day? But at this point providence intervened, in the form of a large hole in the asphalt caused by the severe winter. Petya lost control of the wheel and a stolid Russian birch took the minibus into its embrace.

The burned-out hulk of the Gazelle made one think of the great mercy of God: the lads had suffered nothing more than fright. Well, perhaps more than fright: their community brethren were so indignant that the perpetrators were given categorical instructions to not leave Kitezh, to give up drinking and to work under adult supervision. In addition, Petya was relieved of his driver's licence of which he had been immensely proud.

In one sense, Petya and his brother Misha are adults. At twenty-four and twenty-three, respectively, they have developed their own world views and have attained the right to determine their own lives and futures. After reaching the age of majority, they had chosen to remain at Kitezh, and in doing so had committed to living according to the community's rules and principles.

But in another sense, the brothers are still children. On this occasion, at least, they had chosen to revert to their previous ways by drinking vodka and breaking the rules. They are prepared to work but not to plan their own working day or take responsibility for the outcome of their labour. They still need the rules and structure of the community to live by. We have found that if we don't assign them new tasks, compelling them, from time to time, to broaden their horizons and develop new skills—

making, in effect, their lives a little less easy-going—they would be content to wind up as their biological parents had.

The episode illustrates the challenges inherent in overcoming negative programming in early childhood even after years of living in a therapeutic environment. How negative? Consider the grimness and desperation of Misha and Petya's early youth as revealed in the following conversation I had with Petya in 2003:

Dimitry: What are your first memories?

Petya: On my fifth birthday this boy taught me to smoke as a kind of present. That's one of my first memories. I had to repeat Year Three because of my first love. I used to hang around in the park with the kids from my class. Then I remember my father drinking a lot and he used to say he would kill my mother. It felt like papa never stopped punishing mama, and that's why she went away for a few days. Then she came back, picked us up, and we ran away through this forest.

Dimitry: When did the horrible things start in your life? When did your life start turning nasty?

Petya: I was ten and in Year Four when I really stopped caring about school. I had loads of friends. They were all older than me. They taught me to smoke and how to be cool. Even sitting in class at school, I was always desperate for the moment when I could run out and have a fag with them. I used to drink watered-down vodka every night at the flat of one of the younger policemen. On Saturdays we used to hang out with him outside the disco and he'd give us vodka.

Dimitry: Are you serious?

Petya: Yeah. When I was ten I used to drink vodka outside a disco with a policeman. I was never at home, hardly ever. We lived with my mother's brother as well as their sister and father. When my grandmother died my uncle blamed my mama saying she had poisoned her own mother with vodka. Then my mother met some guy and moved in with him. When we lived with this new 'papa' I completely stopped going to school. I never went home either.

Dimitry: Describe your memories to me.

Petya: I refused to acknowledge this guy my mother got together with. He was scared I would kill him. Can you imagine? When he was drunk he would shout at my mother that he was scared of me. Then he chucked me and my brother out of his house anyway. At first I'd take my rucksack and pretend that I was going to school. Then once, I left my rucksack at home. He looked in it and found I had a knife. When I came home, my mother was waiting for me outside to warn me not to go in.

Dimitry: How did you feel then?

Petya: Nothing. I was relieved if anything. A family's a family, but he wasn't my father. Mama ran to a friend of hers. I started to live on the street. I'm not bitter about it now and I wasn't then, as far as I can remember. I saw it like the whole world is black and white and I'm the only one in colour. Everything that happened, happened because of me. I don't blame anyone. For the first month, my brother and I lived on the streets with a couple of friends. Nobody touched us. What was good was that Mama got a job at the town bakery. We used to go up and get free bread. Then we wanted a change. We started stealing ducks and chickens, digging up people's potatoes. Lots of people helped us, gave us food, they felt sorry for us, but of course some of the locals got fed up with our stealing. They even accused us of shoplifting in the supermarket but that was honestly not us.

Dimitry: Were you proud of yourself?

Petya: Of course I was. I thought everybody else was a wimp. The other kids my age were scared of me; I used to scare them away with a cigarette in my mouth. Fair enough: most of the big lads used to beat me up. I was only ten, after all. Sometimes when I was drunk, they used to beat me up properly.

I recall the first time I saw Petya and Misha. Our only reliable friend at that time was the chief of the Criminal Investigations Department for the Baryatino region, a man everyone respectfully called Dmitrich. Dmitrich told me about two orphans at the Baryatino School who refused to study and were unmanageable, stealing and running away repeatedly. 'It's been decided to take them to an orphanage in Kaluga tomorrow,' he told me. 'Either take them yourself right now or we will send them to the orphanage.'

'Here it is!' I thought to myself, with some anxiety. 'All my uncertainties have been brought to an end by fate knocking on the door. The first children have come to us.' All of Baryatino knew about these brothers, and if we could only manage to do something with them, we could melt the town's icy distrust. I set off through the frost to the garage to start up the old UAZ minibus, having decided that if it didn't start, then such was fate; it wasn't meant to be. Contrary to custom, however, the minibus started instantly. My fate had been determined by the turn of a key.

They brought Petya and Misha into the headmistress' office, and I immediately was struck by these small, thin boys, clothed in identical tracksuits, with short-cropped hair and tears in their eyes. They clearly did not want to engage in dialogue. The headmistress stood next to me and was the only person in the room who stayed calm and in control of the situation. The boys were afraid of me and I was afraid of the boys—or rather, of the choice I had made.

'Children, here is the headmaster of Kitezh, Dimitry Vladimirovitch,' the headmistress told them. 'He is prepared to have you live in his village. If you do not want to, we will send you to Kaluga. Choose now.'

I spoke up, rather unconfidently. 'We only have a few families, three houses,' I told them. 'You'll have to light the stove, carry water, and study. Do you want to go with me?' They looked at me with teary eyes and nodded in silence.

That was all there was to it. In those days the process was simple: there were no papers to fill out, no medical examinations. I don't even recall who filled in the documentation as their foster parents. We had no time or need for formalities then. It was all the same to the boys. All adults had one face for them then, and that face inspired fear.

Goodness, how afraid I was myself in those first years, when we were building Kitezh! When I looked at the closed, silent, sometimes aggressive but more typically introverted children who came to us, I wondered which approach would be best. They had emerged from bullying and totalitarian environments and that is what they understood. I wanted something completely different.

OUR NAIVETÉ

In my imagination, there would be flickering candlelight. Golden specks of light would twinkle in attentive eyes. Enveloped by silence, someone would be reading his favourite poem. The others would listen, enraptured. Then a conversation would ensue about art, personal calling, the conflict between individual and societal interests, or any number of other important topics.

From what romantic source did such a vision come to me? Why did it push me time and time again to gather everyone around me and try to engage them in a philosophical discussion of poetry and higher things, when their focus was on baser things?

How distant that dream was from reality in those first few years. I recall asking Petya in those early years what he wanted most of all.

'To satisfy my needs,' he replied. 'To smoke and have my own freedom.'

'Stas,' I asked another child, 'what did you want most of all when you were in Year Four?'

'To be left alone,' was his reply.

We wanted to awaken twelve-year-old abandoned children to a love of poetry; instead, they would flee from us at every chance, mostly to the forest. They weren't interested in respecting us; they just wanted a break from the pressure—to smoke and talk about their 'real' problems.

My mistake was trying to elevate them to a philosophical level when they still didn't feel even a modicum of security. The more we scolded them, the more they wanted to do what they pleased and the more distant that magical poetry corner became. It called to mind a memorable quote: 'if you lead a man into the kingdom of heaven to whom everything in heaven is foreign, he will be in hell. If you take a man who hates music to a concert, he will fidget from boredom and irritation, and the kindness you showed in taking him there won't make him feel any better.'

One intelligent girl who grew up in Kitezh once asked me, 'Didn't it upset you that the children were scared of you?'

Yes, it upset me. It still upsets me that I was such a fool back then. I didn't see even the most obvious things that were right in front of me.

As I am writing this, Kitezh has been in existence for fifteen years. All of those years have been filled with continuous struggle with children's reluctance to change anything. (I mean anything: they would object even to improvements to the dinner menu or to new films.) Most surprising, however, was their continued insistence on their right to be fearful and distrustful. They could not believe they could change themselves or their lives.

If I was alone with a child I might be able to engage their

interest for a time, but as soon as they were with the other children, they would combine their individual world views to piece together a mosaic of pessimism. They learned from each other that nobody cares a whit about helping others and that the only thing worth striving for is earning lots of money. My attempts to convince them otherwise led to nothing. They simply trusted their own experience.

I should have known: people can't pursue their higher aspirations when their basic needs are not satisfied. What kind of poems will they be engaged by, what kind of philosophical discussions will they have, when all of their experiences have beaten into them the belief that opening up to others is dangerous, that trusting people is dangerous, that relaxing is dangerous? How can some romantic drivel about humanity, harmony, and man's higher calling compete with that kind of experience?

GROWING UP IN THE JUNGLE

A hunter dressed in animal skins creeps through the jungle. His senses are on alert. His bare feet lightly touch the ground under-neath him. His clenched fist clasps his spear. His nostrils quiver as he inhales, analysing the scents around him. His ears are pricked as he listens—is that the rustling of a predatory footstep? He is totally absorbed with his senses and permits no distracting thoughts; if he did, he would be lost. This is what his genes tell him. In the Stone Age, it was only this kind of man—alert, focused, and decisive—who survived.

Petya and Misha are walking around Baryatino. Their senses are alert and their eyes wide open. The world around them is a danger zone; it does not forgive the faint of heart. Over there sits a drunk: he could start swearing at you aggressively or beat you for your last kopecks. A brick lying nearby would help in that situation. 'I can knock a drunk over from ten metres,' brags Misha.

Petya keeps quiet. He's older and knows that it's safer to say nothing.

People are filling a lorry with loaves in front of the bakery. It smells so good. Don't forget to check the back door, in case you can pocket some. Some guy appears in uniform. His whole body is tense, like he's ready to throw you into the bushes. The boys didn't manage to react in time, got caught, and were taken to a children's home.

Petya and Misha walk around their village like it's a jungle. Their minds are as sharp as the hunter's spear. They have no time to think about God, parliaments, or democratic society. They need to think about where their next meal is coming from and where they won't get punched. Getting sidetracked is putting oneself at risk, so they don't.

'I even went to school until Year Five and I wasn't bad,' Misha recalled many years later. 'Then they sent me to a detention centre because of stealing. How could I not steal? I was hungry. Begging is so shameful. In the centre you got beaten for doing something wrong. Then, when I came out, I couldn't make myself think about schoolwork. It hurt my brain.'

Of course his brain hurt. Sine graphs and irregular verbs can scarcely be squeezed into a consciousness brimming with pain and fear. The muses are silent while cannons roar.

He knew the path to happiness and wouldn't allow himself to be distracted by our stupid ideas. We couldn't convince him otherwise. No matter how we tried, we couldn't make him understand that the path to happiness is much, much more complicated.

On the level of sheer existence that Misha was preparing for, his illusions in no way prevented him from living 'normally' within the society whose image he carried in his subconscious. Not knowing how the world was created or how the human body functions does not hinder survival in our modern urban jungles. What if you want to break out of the jungle? For that, Cinderella has to genuinely want to go to the ball.

Misha's spheres of consciousness were like Russian dolls, inserted one within another. He lived in Kitezh, but his consciousness lingered somewhere in his native village. He knew he could not trust anyone and that there was no need to study because it wouldn't help him survive. Some of the convictions of these young people have no basis in reality or bear any connection to the laws of nature; their outlook is despairingly primitive. But then, people once believed that the Earth was flat and still lived and coped with life and solved their everyday, essential problems.

At school in Kitezh, Misha and Petya started to fill in the gaps in their scientific map of the world. But the direction of Misha's fate hardly showed any changes. He still didn't want to know anything beyond what he absolutely had to. He didn't like working very much, he ignored school as far as he could, and he went into the army simply because he didn't know what else to do with his life.

We had to come to terms with the reality that our vision of raising the minds and imaginations of our children with lofty thoughts and inspirational poetry would have to be put on hold while other, darker, corners were explored.

2

Our Image of the World

Parenting means interaction. In order for your influence to get through, you must know, at the very least, where your child, the object of your interaction, is located. He is not located in the room in front of your literal eyes, or in your heart, but in his own world, which, in our view, is identical to his consciousness. The borders of this world, as perceived by the child himself in the first years of life, are located within the limits of the room.

For us, it is simply a room, with wallpaper that, through habit, one ceases to notice, but for him it is a world that is populated by fairies, gnomes, and terrifying monsters. For the child it is precisely these essences, invisible to you and created by his consciousness, that are a thousand times more real than the world beyond the window.

You ceased to notice the sharp edges of the furniture long ago but in the child's world, they are unbearable. They can wait in ambush, then move forward, attack unexpectedly, and implant a bruise before skulking away again. You don't notice the walls and mentally move through them into the network of streets, absorbed by thoughts of work or a holiday in the country; but for a young child they are the portal to a virtual reality of hidden fears and fantasies. In the twilight, the stain on the wall radiates a threat; in the morning, the crystal edges of the vase inspire hope.

Why is it so important for parents to recognise this? Because it is precisely in this world that is closed to us that a child receives his life experiences and it will long be so, if not forever. I will explain schematically. Something occurs in the physical world—say the child drops a cup. The event triggers something in your consciousness and you shout at him but you have engaged him in a dialogue without considering what might be happening in his consciousness. It is possible that in his world he is making a monumental discovery—the universal law of gravity—but having received in the process an emotional injury, he abandons that discovery and retreats to the level of emotional reaction, closing off questions of how and why and retaining only the memory of pain and fear. Frequently it is impossible to perceive why a child is happy or upset: to follow the chain of stimulus and reaction. In his private world, a child is concerned with interpretation. He compares an event with previous experiences and impressions he derives from fairy tales, films, the observations of peers and, if you are lucky, your own explanations. In every person's consciousness a personal image of the world coalesces from childhood.

A simple peasant sees his environment in a way that differs from the wise man who is more able to perceive the hidden links between things and phenomena and see the flow of energy behind events. Hence when we say that people have different world views, it means that a person doesn't deal with this world but with a model created in his own consciousness based on what his senses tell him about the outer world and how his reason has processed that information.

The basis of an individual's image of the world is laid down in early childhood, from his or her earliest experienced feelings—interaction with mother, swaddling, games, and so forth. Over these simple feelings more complex ones are laid and arranged in a chain of interconnections, linking objects with knowledge of what to do with them. I was hungry, I cried, I was fed. Gradually a child spreads a web of cause and effect that encompasses the entire world that he can perceive with his senses. This is his image of the world .

The same phenomenon can be described with various terms and images. I find it helpful to consider the layout of consciousness using the categories suggested by Russian ethno-psychologist A. A. Shevtsov, founder of the Academy of Self-Knowledge. In essence he constructs a theory of self-knowledge based on practical popular psychology. He offers the following scheme for the creation of one's image of the natural and social worlds:

A child starts at birth to perceive the natural world with his body. He crawls around the house, bumps against sharp corners, leans against solid objects, pricks and cuts himself. Information about the natural world is gathered through pain in various parts of his body. As long as he has a body, this information will be in his consciousness. From the moment of birth, the blanks of his consciousness start to be filled with unsorted information in its simplest forms.

Having bumped his body painfully several times (or having run into a wall, been burned, slapped, shouted at), the child learns that extremely undesirable effects can come from without. This 'from without' turns out to be his main discovery, forcing the child to feel the boundary between himself and the outer world.

A child can only think by creating various sequences of images out of extremely simple impressions that were implanted in his memory at an earlier stage. A.A. Shevtsov calls them 'primary images'. One might compare the process of basic impressions joining into more complex combinations with a molecule that links with other simple complimentary molecules. Information received later on is either understood and included in the logical sequence of things, or it is rejected.

One of the first basic pieces of information is the experience of encountering a solid object. For example, in the image of the world of every person on this planet, water is present and everyone knows what to do with it. You could say this knowledge is implanted in a person's primary images. When we are thirsty, we don't even consider what we should do. We simply drink, since our life has depended on this from the first moments of our existence.

Which primary images are implanted in us before birth is a question of inquiry and debate. I am inclined to believe that a child is born with a certain programme that, at the very least, colours the way initial experience is interpreted.

There follows endless instinctive processing of impressions received from touching, playing, washing and placing these impressions in one's memory, the storage place for our consciousness, to serve as building material for the later construction of more complex chains.

Each of us is engaged from birth in a very serious task: the formation in one's consciousness of a model of the world that reflects reality. Consciousness can be likened to the operating system of a new computer. When a child is born he already has consciousness, but it is a space waiting to be filled with information—like installing new programmes and documents. In this model, in the consciousness of the child these first images and events are linked together like Lego bricks to create a whole image of the child's world. These bricks are building an image of the world that is not the reality, but the child is testing how to behave in reality and to discover his best options.

Any change in his surrounding reality leads to changes in the child's image of the world—that imprint, that reflection of reality, which with maturity becomes a working programme. It is precisely this programme, constructed out of chance interactions that will define the individual's view of the world—his reactions, dreams and ambitions. As elemental internal forces develop, they demand the expansion of consciousness in all directions but the increasing experience of pain places ever more obstacles in the way of that expansion, just as worms eat cavities in a growing apple.

On the basis of this model, a child soon becomes capable of anticipating his environment and learns which behaviour will achieve an objective, such as crying when his wet nappy needs changing or smiling and cooing to engage his mother's interest.

Usually, we think in blocks of ideas, simultaneously perceiving an object and the signal from our memory files telling us what we should do with this object. In this way we learn to act rationally and not waste time and strength on useless contemplation. Saving time and strength allows us to survive in the world. From these blocks, tested by our own experience, an image of the world is created in our consciousness. Again using the metaphor of a computer, one might say that say that every person has in his consciousness a programme that calculates various scenarios and with it plays out all possible courses of action, and their consequences, before acting.

The child who succeeds with little effort in obtaining food and attention through cooing or crying learns quickly that it is worth investing effort and will power in the great world surrounding him. This means he will continue to seek ways of making an effort to achieve what he wants. Conversely, the child who is forced to scream for hours without a desired outcome is likely to subconsciously impose a ban on any useless expression of will. In this case, the very operating system of the consciousness is already full of viruses, and the images of interrelationships in human society will be distorted as a result.

If a child is beaten and left unfed and changed, impressions of solid objects representing pain and fear, worry and danger, are lodged at the base of the model that he will use in the future to process his actions. From such initial images—fire means hot (and painful or dangerous), water will quench your thirst—the child's mind creates, as it gains experience, a long chain of dependencies, which can distort his image of the world.

If a child is loved, he absorbs the ability to interact and interpret 'from his mother's milk'. As he grows, he will learn new words and learn to think according to the generally accepted worldview that those words represent. Whatever new ideas a child assimilates, however, they remain affected by the primary ideas and images he assimilated in the first months of life. He may like to sit with his father near the fire, which will create an image for him of the warmth of the hearth, but inside this image, the instinctive knowledge that fire is pain will also be preserved. In the same way, a natural born child will always remember that his parents were feeding and protecting him from the very beginning and even when he grows up and argues with parents, this initial image of love and connection maintains that inner contact. Orphans usually will not have this initial image if they lost their parents too early or if they were abused during the first days of their lives. It is probably in those initial interactions that the code that makes the child a part of humanity is implanted. Thrown to the wolves, a human infant absorbs primary images into his consciousness that can turn him into a wolf.

In ancient times the natural world presented humanity with pressing necessities and urgent tasks to survive but in present times, threatening beasts and natural disasters have lost their power and ability to engage us. The natural world has been reduced to the size of a television screen for most of us but other dangers have come to the fore. For a civilised person, it is extremely important to find the safe paths—the metaphorical feeding places and hunting grounds that exist in the social world.

RESENTMENT AND THE 'BODY OF TRUTH'

After separating physically from the mother, the child continues to live in the sphere of her consciousness. A child is never alone; he is always part of a system. He grows and begins to stretch the borders of his unseen body in the parents' sphere of consciousness, claiming an ever greater part of it. To avoid going mad, the parents are forced to resist, and not allow the child to occupy their attention fully and keep him within defined boundaries. At first this is done unconsciously, then intentionally—'Don't act up; don't shout; go to bed, I'm working.'

The child begins to learn to speak and curiosity drives him to lengthen his journeys into the surrounding world, where he discovers new people and a new living environment. In this environment knowledge and observance of convention is of the first importance, and for that one requires speech.

Leaving the maternal cocoon, the child enters the world of human interrelations, into an environment woven from the fields of consciousness of the people around him. The wellbeing of the developing individual depends on his ability to determine the quality of these hidden fields. Of course, in the initial stages the child is unable to differentiate sharp edges or solid obstacles. As a result, he bruises himself and experiences pain that teaches him the limits of his body. This body is already limited by the field of conventions, expectations and injuries that interaction with the surroundings brings him. One could say that around every child there exists another 'body of truth' with which he constantly grasps your observations, instructions, and even bad jokes. Knowing that this other body exists, you can gradually learn to discern the nuances of mood and feeling that one cannot always describe.

'At fifteen I understood that my parents were lying to me: the world is not as they use to describe it to me.'

'I understood that no one loves me and no one needs me.'

'I reject the rotten values of your false society.'

There is nothing surprising about this reaction. The young person has simply started to use his brains for the first time and has seen the complexity of the surrounding world. He has become scared. It is scary to enter adult existence—simply to admit that the battle for life could be beyond his capabilities. Then a compensatory mechanism kicks in—a search for the guilty party. One has to get by, after all. To not lose one's self-respect and avoid the battle, one has to find those to blame for one's weakness. Very often, the parent fills that role.

We can only redeem a child by helping him to change his image of the world—to purge it of viruses that prevent him from seeing reality. This realisation precipitated a new stage in Kitezh's development. We became a therapeutic community, concentrating on creating an environment in which those in our care could develop.

3

The Origins of Kitezh

I am often asked what Kitezh is and how I first conceived of it. Is it a cooperative community of foster families, an attempt to rejuvenate the Russian tradition of the community, an effort to change our way of life or some kind of spiritual venture?

I'm not sure I really know. It took some years for the idea of Kitezh to grow within me, as gradually and naturally as a shoot sprouting from the earth. Time passed and the tiny seedling germinated, the sprout burst through to the light, broke away from the seed, and began to grow with a force of its own, revelling in the sun and withstanding battering by the rain and the wind.

At first I dreamed, or rather I sensed that I would not be able to give my life to the quest for material wealth; that possessing things, a career, and even happy idleness would be a waste of effort in the short snippet of the Earth's journey that is my life. I felt then, and know now, that there is nothing higher for mankind than to see himself as a part of the cosmos, to love and to be loved, to do good by learning, and to make an effort. I felt that I would not be alone on that path because, after all, these are simple truths, and however cloudy they may seem, they are to be found everywhere and by everyone who looks. You need only to create the necessary conditions for your life to become a path that can embody the will of the Creator. It is not competition but love that is the primary source of creative energy.

Kitezh

I was born during the Khrushchev era, studied history during Brezhnev's rule and began working as a journalist at the height of the years of stagnation. I would come to look back on this later period as a golden age. It is no surprise, therefore, that ideas of revolution and collectivism were fundamental to my worldview. It was only later, after I had analysed history and accumulated life experiences of my own, that I realised that my outlook on the world was very far from reality.

When Gorbachev came to power and ushered in *perestroika*, everything that I had only considered in my most vague theoretical musings suddenly became possible. I saw that my new outlook on the world was wholly compatible with reality. I was more experienced by then and I could see that appearances can be deceptive and that there was probably something more real behind what I had thought was reality. When I was at school and university I had become accustomed to believing in the party leadership. I had come to believe that the world would be made happier if we could solve political and economic problems. Now I understand that the inner realities of each individual depends to a far greater extent on the way he or she is brought up, on the system of values on which that upbringing was based, which may or may not correspond to those of the word around us. I was fortunate enough to have very good parents. My mother was a professor of medicine and my father was an officer. They invested enough in me to ensure that I did not become totally disillusioned when the communist system collapsed. Nor did I believe blindly in the advertisements that promised the abundance of capitalism, and I was not ready to accept Michael Jackson as my new hero.

In school I was a poor student, but I read avidly, immersing myself in books on all topics like a swimmer in the sea. I entered Moscow State University's Institute of the Countries of Asia and Africa, one of the most prestigious institutes in the USSR, which provided me with a stomach ulcer, the chance to participate in student theatre, and a trip to India. This latter experience entered my consciousness with the red colour of loamy soil and the thick scent of incense and cow dung. At the bottom of an ocean of memories, I can still locate a stone temple in the shape of a pyramid with a sharply peaked top. The temple stood on the outskirts of Madras and in it was a priest who knew the wisdom of the ancients. I entered this world with an open mind that was already so exposed and pliable that merely one drop of new information could instantly dissolve all of the entrenched modes of thought put in place in previous years. The magic of India opened within the consciousness of a Soviet student the prospect of other worlds.

My parents raised me as a communist, in that I always believed in communal values and never wanted to become rich. My mother, a scientist, somehow managed to implant in me a germ of curiosity and she taught me to believe my own ideas more than ideological propaganda. The biggest discovery I made in India was that another reality existed beside our Soviet reality in which people managed to live and be happy and feel it was a natural way of life.

There I met Svyatoslav Rerich, the son of the renowned Russian artist, philosopher and traveller, Nicholas Rerich. Svyatoslav lived in Bangalore on his own estate. Every Russian tourist and official sought an audience with him. So did I. For the first time in my life I met a man absolutely different from those I was used to, even at Moscow University. He was a remnant of a Russian culture that had expired. He found time to show a young student his paintings and to talk with me about religion, the future of the world, and the mysteries of the Himalayas. At that moment, I felt that if such a person existed, then there must be others like him representing a different reality, and that I must do my best to become one of them. I was twenty at that time, so I was sure it would happen sooner or later. With the self-confidence of youth I had no doubt that the time would surely come and I would be called to this other reality.

I returned to the Soviet Union with this new image of the world implanted in me. I was not critical of Soviet reality nor had any inner conflict at that time because I thought it was just a matter of time, knowledge and career that the change would happen. Ten years later, when I was thirty, I did begin to understand that if I wanted another reality I would have to create it myself. There were no good, kind wizards to create the new world for me and invite me to join them. Now as I approach fifty, I see that the organisation of Kitezh became a matter of inner survival. My new image of the world acquired in India pushed me to make an effort, for otherwise I would lose it, but at that time I simply went to work as a journalist at Russian State Radio, Mayak, without conflict or dissatisfaction.

In the summer of 1982 the State Committee for Television and Broadcasting sent me to work as a leader in a Pioneer camp, the Russian version of a Boy Scout summer camp. Strangely enough, I liked the experience. When I returned to Moscow after forty chaotic days, I felt so lost and lonely that I wept. The children's problems and sorrows had made a deep impression on my consciousness. Thereafter I went to the camp every year simply because I could not bring myself to abandon them.

The children grew older and the world around them became more complicated and dangerous. They asked the kind of important and penetrating questions for which I, a young and self-assured graduate and journalist specialising in international affairs, simply could not find answers, but I was still young and naïve enough to think deeply and honestly about their questions.

The children loved me, but as it turned out, I was powerless to alter their fates. Fourteen-year-old Lora had a gift for drawing. She was very interesting to talk to. She reacted with animation to all that went on around her and was drawn towards adult society but when her parents divorced, she found comfort among a group of hippies who gathered by the Gogol monument on the Boulevard Ring in central Moscow. She stopped going to school because the great changes in her life left no place for the grey ordinariness of her past. A year later, she started taking drugs. Two years later, she was a mere shadow of her former self. Volodya was an extremely bright and aware adolescent. When his father abandoned his family, Volodya stopped studying. He was part of my group at camp for four years, and he told me that I was like a substitute father for him. We talked at length about life, but all the same, he turned to alcohol and I could not do a thing. I could not save a soul.

Seeing how selfish and weak parents destroy the lives of their children and how school, the Komsomol organisation (the Young Communist League), and other elements of our state crush the individual fates of those who lacked support or faced setbacks early in life, I became all the more aware of my own helplessness.

I worked in the camp as a leader for ten years, summer and winter. After receiving my doctoral degree, I was appointed special international correspondent for the Mayak Radio Network.

Years later, after repeatedly analysing the historical process and acquiring my own life experience, I understood that my world view, though conducive to success at work and in the Komsomol, was only remotely linked to reality. What was going on in society and in families was strikingly different from the message I was delivering in all sincerity to the two hundred million people who tuned into the network. I am not referring to allegiance to the Socialist regime or devotion to the ideas of Marx and Lenin, but to something more essential, a certain fundamental understanding of the world. Was my world real? Why do people live as they do? Why do I go to work? Why do I exist at all? These questions did not occur to me spontaneously, but rather as the result of reflecting upon my childhood and reconsidering the processes I had always assumed to be natural.

Reviewing my own childhood programming first led me to think that other people were also programmed in childhood and, second, that their programmes also could be changed. For more than fifteen years, I unconsciously attempted to understand where inside my body was I and where was the programme that the surrounding world had put inside me during childhood. What in this programme did I like, what did I dislike, and, most important, why did I have to carry out a programme that society implanted into me without asking my opinion?

I was too young at the time, of course, to have been consulted, but as I became older, I started to question even the commonly accepted aphorism that 'it is impossible to live in society and be free from society'. I began to recognise how many distinct societies function freely and well within Russia. Then I asked: Would it not be possible to choose the society in which I would like to live and become the master of my own life programme? For me, these long-term efforts to gain understanding of my own programme turned out to be such a useful and fascinating activity that it eventually became my favourite instrument for rehabilitative work with troubled children and the adults I was close to.

I began to imagine an ideal place for bringing up children. I had just finished reading *The Glass Bead Game* by Herman Hesse when the solution struck me like a bolt of lightning: a province devoted to education! The Castalian Spring! By this time, I had already visited India, Vietnam, Mongolia and the countries of Eastern Europe. My lack of professional training in education allowed me to take an unbiased look at my Pioneer camp experience and combine it with the historical experience of Russia, European civilisation and the Orient.

We often say that that we cannot understand each other—that our world views, faiths, and dreams are incompatible with the ways of life, traditions and beliefs of others in the Occident and Orient, but these incompatibilities exist only in the human mind. One must realise that everything in the world exists together and flows into and around everything else in the seamless interconnectedness and continuity of human history. Contradictions appear only in the worldview of individuals enclosed within the confines of the programmes they were given by their parents or their cultural and historical conditioning. This means it is possible to make use of everything human civilisation has brought into the world, though it is important to be creative in using these gifts of world culture without changing our unique essence—without ceasing to be Russian.

When Gorbachev came to power and *perestroika* became state policy, everything began to seem possible. I left journalism and, with the support of the Mayak radio network, led a series of charity radio marathons to raise money for my fantastic programme. Russia in the early nineties was beginning to move towards a free market economy, making it possible to construct my social model on entirely legal foundations. Acting pragmatically, I took advantage of the situation. In 1992, I left behind my job, my apartment in Moscow, my *dacha* (summer house) outside the city, and all ambitions of a career within a society suddenly aspiring to liberal values, and moved to the little village of Chumazovo (which translates as Dirty Face) in an isolated corner of the Kaluga region some three hundred kilometres south of Moscow. There I dedicated myself to the creation of my own little island of reality. I named it Kitezh, after the mythical Russian city made famous by the Rimsky Korsakov opera, which sank beneath the waters of a great lake but was foretold to rise once more in Russia's darkest hour to herald the dawn of a new age.

Back in 1992, I honestly did not know what I was dreaming about. I was simply in a state of creative insanity as if I were not carrying out my own plans but obeying a command from above. In this world no mortal can be the master of a process that is intertwined with the surrounding environment. As Goethe wrote, 'We can leap off mountains, but many factors subsequently intervene, including the law of gravity, the strength of the wind, the density of the material on which we land, and such hard-to-perceive concepts as luck and fortune. The first step is ours, but afterwards, everything depends on the will of the elements—on physical and metaphysical laws.'

I entered a state of utter infatuation with my idea. It was as if a stream of energy was flowing through me, concentrating all my thoughts and forces on the singular focus of my dream. I even chose the name without hesitation. Every thought, every movement of my mind, was a step towards the creation of my village. I imagined the faces of my collaborators, devised the rules of the community, sketched the houses, and contrived financial schemes. I was in a state of total concentration that would permit neither a turning back nor the renunciation of what I had resolved to do. I could not permit myself the luxury of wasting energy on doubts. When I gave up my profession and began living in a hut amidst abandoned fields and the remains of the pre-Revolutionary estate, it did not occur to me that what I was doing was difficult (or, as many said, foolish). I allowed no thoughts that were unrelated to the fulfillment of my dream. I moved towards my goal and saw only the goal; everything else was rejected. Even the amount of strain and insults I had to endure didn't bother me at all. Everything seemed so simple in those early years.

PUTTING THEORY INTO PRACTICE

In the beginning, Kitezh was an empty field and an idea— scratchings on a piece of slate. I had no clear plan; only a vague sense of what it must be. The details, I thought, would come in the process. Now I know this was the best way. At that time I knew of at least twenty other efforts to start intentional communities in Russia. Not one of them survives today. Why? Because their founders had elaborate plans and worked with those plans, not with reality. Like the very first prehistoric aquatic creature that crawled from the sea, it had to have a goal, but it also had to make the effort on its own, feeling with its soft body every stone and grain of sand and adapting that body to the requirements for survival. Its efforts generated energy and that energy changed its very being. A similar phenomenon occurs with our children. They are changing every day by meeting problems and challenges. That is why one must not just build a community, but grow it and let it evolve.

The original idea was to create ideal conditions for the development and education of abandoned children. For the idea to acquire a material form, we needed people to come and live with us who were ready to serve the idea, and for them the first things we needed were houses, roads and electricity—the practical necessities of living.

For the first year, things proceeded quite smoothly. I acquired forty hectares of land in the Baryatino region in the Kaluga district because at that time there was plenty of land that nobody wanted. People who had heard my inspired call to arms on national radio came from all corners of Russia to start a new life in the name of a higher purpose. Having received adequate donations of money and building materials to construct our first houses, we got up early and worked until late, hurrying to get the roofs on before the snows came. After our day was finished, we sang songs around a campfire surrounded by our tents, making plans about how we were going to live as one big family raising children, reading books, making beautiful artifacts, and existing in harmony with nature and our neighbours.

Imagine our joy on New Year's Eve of 1994 when fifteen of us—joined by another twenty-two who had volunteered during the summer and had left their flats in Moscow and Kaluga to be with us—celebrated the first year of our grand experiment of living in one finished and two almost finished houses. Surrounded by snowbound and uninhabited forests and fields, we truly felt like creators of a new world. As golden candlelight flickered in frosty windows, we revelled in the joy of being together and were profoundly grateful that our efforts were starting to bear fruit.

We used conventional psychological tests to select those open to interaction with others, with a creative attitude to life. After a trial period, a group of people who were to become the teaching staff was selected. Every community member became a foster parent, a teacher and a mentor except those who worked as volunteers. The most difficult task was to raise enough money to build the houses and dress and feed the children.

It is natural for man to make mistakes. During any historical period in Russia, raising money for charity has never been a simple matter. I really didn't imagine that I would be investing my life's savings into setting up Kitezh, or that what I wanted to do would be going against the mindset of society, economic reality or the flaws of human nature.

For example, John, a great optimist and master with his hands, and his wife took to drink—not from disillusionment or despair but an inability to cope with deep emotions. The farmers in the local villages drank in a truly Russian way; many drank regularly out of despair. Their lives were without the slightest cause for joy. We couldn't imagine that this epidemic could infect our community.

Another Kitezhan, Nikolai, who had worked as a businessman in St Petersburg, could not suppress his enterprising nature. Suddenly we discovered that he had been selling trainers off the back of a lorry in the local market. He was not a bad person; he simply didn't understand the importance in a community of consulting with others before acting. Kitezh was a strange creature to the locals. They thought us foreign and incomprehensible and would spy on us. Imagine their reaction when word circulated that we were involved with black market trainers!

We didn't have enough money, often, not even enough for food. Out of desperation, we sometimes had to trade a bottle of vodka to borrow a tractor or cajole the local peasants to help with raising a roof or building a chimney. We were also born of this world, and to break away from its laws was no easier than it is for a blade of grass to break through asphalt. Fortunately, I understood then the importance of learning to wait. The time comes for everything: for every person and for every community.

This is the story of how at thirty-three, beginning with a tiny plot of land, I began to cultivate the dream of Kitezh. I sowed the seed of my dream in the soil of reality and watered it with the sweat of my labour. As Goethe said, nothing else was within my power. Kitezh is growing through its own will. Whenever I am asked if Kitezh resembles my initial vision, I am at a loss for words. It seems not to. That is how it should be. That is only human. That is simply how the world works.

4

Unfamiliar Territory

Here is what a number of Kitezh children have had to say about their past:

I arrived in Kitezh when I was nine years old. Before that I lived in an orphanage, having left my home at four. My father was put in prison and my mother turned to drink to deal with her problems and eventually just forgot about me. After that I remember living with some old man and woman who fed me once a day on rotten fish and were always drunk. One day the old man stabbed the old woman with a knife; she was dying before my very eyes. Blood was flowing down on to the floor and the drunken old man ordered me to clean it up. Soon the police came and took me off to an orphanage. To this day I sometimes wake up in the night from nightmares about this time in my life. I see the scene with the blood and feel helpless. In Kitezh I have tried to forget the past. Kitezh is a completely different world. It's much warmer, more comfortable. I know that my past will always be with me but I will do my best not to go back to it.

I was often beaten by both my parents but I still loved them. When I was at school with other girls, I never told them about it. I didn't want to be taken from my parents and put in a children's home. But eventually I was put in one. After two years I was taken to Kitezh. At first I couldn't see the difference. Only now, at the age of fourteen, do I know I was lucky. If I hadn't come to live in Kitezh, I know I would be an alcoholic by now, or dead.

When they took me away from my parents and put me in an orphanage it was very painful. Very often I cry at night and remember my father and mother. I thought I would always be with my parents and brothers, that they would always look after me but it didn't turn out that way. I like Kitezh very much and it is like my new family, though I miss my parents and I cannot forget.

According to official statistics, eighty percent of the children who pass through Russian orphanages are unable to deal with the challenges of adult life. Accustomed to the state handing them everything, they cannot find work and are prone to falling in with criminal gangs or succumbing to alcohol or drugs.

This harsh truth demands that we in Kitezh bring up our children so they are prepared to deal with the challenges of real life. For some reason it is difficult for many good people to recognise that the world is capable of destroying those who are not prepared to deal with its challenges. In an ideal world, bringing up a child requires a holistic system that not only offers the complete gamut of life's challenges, but also provides teachers and parents who can decide when the child is prepared to face them and how strong the challenge should be.

For the first five years of Kitezh we were occupied with building houses and a way of life. We believed that the children living in our families and helping us would adopt our ideals naturally. This proved to be an illusion. Although none of them became alcoholics or got involved with criminal gangs, the first three children who grew up with us did not pursue their education further, despite our best hopes for them. It became obvious to us that the majority of abandoned children resist any change in their worldview and don't embrace the necessity to study, learn a profession, or adopt our shared culture.

A child who has suffered violence and abandonment retreats

into a shell. One may be excessively quiet and withdrawn; another may be overly emotional, using hysterics to try to keep at bay the dangers of the outer world. Either way, such children are motivated to protect themselves from the external world; and their mode of self-protection resists any change in their learned responses or a broadening of experience that carries with it the risk of understanding and development. Whether they are five-year-old boys or sixteen-year-old girls, they resist all attempts by adults to shatter their childhood illusions because they are part of their own image of the world. In fact, a person who tries to interfere in their internal world becomes an enemy even though he considers himself a caring parent.

A parent can permit a child to hurt himself, because then his mistakes will be more evident for him. This is the natural way in which development occurs. Children want to make their own mistakes because it is then their own experience, but parents must be careful not to allow this pain to be too severe. The wounds of the soul must be treated immediately otherwise the scars remain.

As described in chapter two, the internal life of a child is unfamiliar territory. Our best guess is that there is some kind of programme within each child by nature that is responsible for the speed and quality of choices that he makes and that may also influence the inferences and discoveries the child makes. Even everyday experience, it would seem, is stored according this inner programme. As with any programme, it can be corrupted by viruses from within (such as fear, anger or envy) and without (by rough handling, for example). Since we don't really know how to correct such errors, we should consciously avoid making them in the first place.

It is much easier to learn computer programming than it is to comprehend the logic of a child's development but computer programming is a highly technical skill done only by talented and well-trained specialists. Parenting comes with no certification requirement or operator's manual. If we have children, we do it, trained specialist or not.

The wealth of discoveries a child makes produces qualitative changes in his view of the world. Every day of a child's life is filled with new discoveries, each of which leaves an indelible impression on his consciousness for life. The old personality doesn't disappear but simply moves inside the new personality like Russian *matryoshka* dolls. Information from the inner dolls rises to the surface when conditions warrant and the person starts to behave according to models from early childhood without any idea where the urge comes from.

CHILDREN OPEN THEIR OWN PATH TO DEVELOPMENT

It was about six months ago that Misha first showed us he could converse in an adult way. This was the second time he had shared his ideas with us. These were his ideas:

I used to be scared to death of my parents and I used to get slapped on the face by my mum and my dad for asking questions. I used to be able to ask Granny about some things, but she was useless and didn't love us.

I've never believed that I could talk to you. When I got to Kitezh I decided I was going to run away the next day. It was only because you left me alone that I decided to stick it out and see if anything interesting happened.

You drummed all this idiotic stuff into my head for three years and my head was close to exploding. I couldn't work or study. Pavel used to beat me and Petya when I couldn't keep up in maths [an exaggeration—DM]. After that we were scared more.

At the school in Kaluga everyone, absolutely everyone, was

mad on drugs and air guns. I don't know why I attract those kind
of people or why they attract me, but I know, if I go to university
then I'll get into drugs again. I mean cannabis or marijuana, not
heroin. At that school, I was a good fighter. There were lots of
fights, but I was always one of the strongest. So why should I do
kung fu with Dimitry?

I get really bored here, so I used to go in to Baryatino to drink.
The others always covered up for me but if I'd had a motorbike
I'd ride at more than one hundred and twenty kilometres per
hour, and then I wouldn't be bored.

You can stop the kids in Kitezh from smoking and taking
drugs if you isolate them from the outside world and make them
work morning to night. It's really boring here; there's nothing to
do in Kitezh.

Here I interrupt him: There are countless things that have
changed in Kitezh in the last five years. Now we have bikes,
computers, trips to other places in Russia and abroad and so
forth. Most kids in Kaluga don't live like that, or in Moscow.

Misha's prediction proved to be wrong. None of the children
at Kitezh started taking drugs. Quite the opposite: all of them
started to read, study, use computers and put on plays. They
suddenly started to find life in Kitezh interesting. Misha entered
the Army with a view of Kitezh that bore no relation to reality but
for him, his view was reality. Misha, why did you not want to
change despite what life was telling you?

When he was left to his own devices in Baryatino, there was a
break in his development and we didn't know how to get this
process going again. He had been used to living without his basic
needs being fulfilled, so he was satisfied when he felt secure and
had enough food and cigarettes. He had decided that nothing else
in life was really necessary or worth the bother.

As Abraham Maslow stresses, for most individuals, most of

the time, basic needs and values take precedence over higher needs and values, which retards the individual's development. Only the healthiest and most mature, well-developed individuals choose higher values, though this is probably because there is a solid basis of satisfied lower needs.

The Kitezh environment did not pose a threat to Misha and he got used to the discomfort that arose from the Teachers Council's dissatisfaction with his schoolwork. (Unlike the whip at the juvenile detention centre, the only physical nuisance he confronted in Kitezh was mosquito bites.) Life didn't put Misha's world outlook in question. In the village, he had friends who confirmed his outlook on things, but his undeveloped psyche and monotonous and rigid habits concealed from him the missing parts in his view of the world and distracted him from life's riddles and doubts. Misha didn't want to know more than what was essential, instinctively sensing that knowing more would complicate life.

The fight for survival forced him to grow a thick shell and he stopped developing inside it. Put another way, Misha grew up too quickly. Things turned out slightly differently for his older brother. This conversation took place when Petya, at twenty, returned from the Army.

Dimitry: Petya, you've put on an act in front of yourself. You've told yourself you have no desire to develop. You succeeded until being in the Army forced you to think about surviving as an independent personality. Only then did you want to scamper quickly like a lizard from a dried up reservoir. You tried to make sense of things. This is what you wrote to me when you were in the Army: 'I can't live without Kitezh. Nobody wants to learn anything here, to talk about anything except grub and vodka. I feel sorry for them. They're scared of life and of the future and they refuse to think about it. Luckily I've got you guys...'

It really pressed down on you and you started to look things in the world that, before, you didn't even know existed. With your increased awareness, your world started to reveal all kinds of interlinking ideas you had never noticed before. You started to see the forces and laws that are usually hidden on the other side of the visible world.

Petya: 'I want to stay in Kitezh and help you help other kids.' The hunter had overcome his own fear and seen reality through the illusion. He had grown up to see that the jungle was just a figment of his imagination and that he needed to help others, not fight them.

NATURE OR NURTURE?

Seven years ago, my wife and I brought our first son, Svyatoslav, home from the hospital. He crawled freely on carpeted floors around the second story of our dwelling and enjoyed strolls around the tree-lined boulevards of a nearby park accompanied by his family—his father, mother, and four adopted brothers and sisters—all of whom behaved tenderly and lovingly toward him at all times.

As an infant and toddler, Svyatoslav was shielded from television, coarse language, and displays of egotism, aggression, or greed. The second story of our house was full of toys. One day, when our little boy was getting tired of his toys, we invited over Nastya, a little girl who had been born into another Kitezh family a couple of months after Svyatoslav, to enjoy his little paradise but something unexpected happened. Svyatoslav got nervous in her presence. He began to dash around on all fours and drag all his toys into a heap in the centre of the room. Grabbing a plastic sabre, he sat perched on top of the pile of toys and shooed away his guest, proclaiming, 'They're mine! I'm not giving you any!'

As the eighteenth century French philosopher and educator Rousseau noted, 'Children do not come *tabula rasa*.' Svyatoslav's behaviour was determined by his internal programme or instincts. Where could this possibly have come from? My wife and I had never discussed or even mentioned the concept of private property or the protection of it, either at home or in the community. Svyatoslav could not possibly have acquired the idea that something belongs to him and that he should need to protect it. There was simply nobody from whom he could have derived such an example. Yet right there in front of me was a concrete fact: that my own son had acted according to the instinctive programme that had manifested itself over and over again throughout human history. The programme already was innately inside of him; it simply activated itself at the first available opportunity. I had previously accepted the possibility that a newborn child could have some innate programme for behaviour. This was vivid confirmation.

It would be tempting to try and 'hack' this programme and alter it, but in its wisdom, nature (or, if you will, the Creator) has concealed the portal to it, guaranteeing to every personality on the planet the inalienable right to freedom of choice. Children are wilful personalities that should not be viewed as the property of their parents. (Poet Kalil Gibran likens them to arrows loosed from the parental bow.) They are born with distinctive sets of talents and aspirations and are capable of their own self-development. Thus, it should not surprise us when they insist upon their right to mould the contours of their future, even at the risk of conflict with their parents. Infantile intellect and emotions feed on life's experience, and the personality develops according to its internal programme, gaining confidence, strength, and experience in self and the surrounding environment. Through overcoming obstacles, the child grows physically in strength and will power.

The loss of parents or the experience of violence or conflict in the family can halt, slow down, or disfigure a child's development. His spirit is afflicted with a kind of disease. It can manifest itself in anger towards the world, a grudge over a real or imagined rejection, the loss of confidence in one's strengths, or any number of other ways. Thus the child is deflected from the path to his own self-realisation.

Who among us parents has not been driven to despair by our children's unpredictability? They will deny perfectly apparent truths and draw what appear to us to be illogical conclusions from our admonitions; perceive our goodness as weakness; and our love as untrue. It is paradoxical that this programme is responsible for the intellectual conclusions the child draws from life's situations. Even twins who are raised in the same environment in the same situation may have a completely different experience.

If we do have a life programme, from where does it come? In his book, *Games People Play*, psychologist Erik Berne, the creator of transactional analysis, traced it back to role-playing with parents, but this theory overlooks evidence that bears witness to the fact that there is often a very powerful programme in abandoned children that is not necessarily taken from their parents.

Because our thirty children in Kitezh come from different cultural and regional influences, they embody the possibility of development beyond the strict roles that are prescribed for them by parents and society. 'If you learn to look inside yourself, you won't get lost,' says Feodor, one of our earlier graduates whose parents died of alcoholism and who is now studying law. 'I learned that from my own experience.'

What if your child pays more attention to a neighbour than you, or dreams of becoming a Hollywood celebrity? It is our wealth of experience that differentiates us from our child, and we try to nudge him to make discoveries. He makes discoveries but draws his own conclusions. I am drawn more to the theory of cleric Anthony Surozhsky—that every human being has the profound ability to change the direction of his life and transform himself.

This does not mean we are doomed to ignorance regarding our children's development and can only pray to higher powers for grace. We have to accept that the question does not have one simple answer. It is tempting to think that I could sell more books if I pulled some formula out of thin air that could be easily understood and accepted. We have a tendency to embrace ideas that are simple to understand. Unfortunately, it has never been easy to explain the laws that rule the human microcosm. In the words of the poet Omar Khayam, 'Man, like the world in the mirror, has many faces. He is nothing and yet he is boundlessly great.'

A child's consciousness is malleable. It is indented every day by new impressions. The new ones replace the old, and there is no way of telling for sure what will be discarded as unimportant, what will resurface years later, and what will transform his view of the world today. This is no insignificant matter. A woman once told me that when she was ten years old she overheard her mother telling a friend that 'my daughter is a means to an end'. Her whole world, which had been built upon love, trust and confidence, was shattered. In its place, she began to experience grief and lack of self-worth. Her mother might have been joking, but her daughter had not yet learned to differentiate between a joke and something said in earnest. As a result, the daughter lost her trust in her mother.

I have no other advice to offer than to urge parents to pay daily attention to changes in your child's world. It is easy to loose track of subtle changes, and you may no longer understand your child's reactions. A real example shows how important it is not to lose children's trust. One child reports: 'Once at teatime mama asked me, "Slavik, do you smoke?" She asked me so quietly and kindly. I considered it and said, "Yes, sometimes". And she started to scream and shout at me… So, basically, for the next ten years I thought it better not to tell the truth.'

When you lose a child's trust, you also lose any possibility of influencing that child's future decisions. The good news is that even if your relationship with your child has been compromised, you can still improve the situation. Your child is emotionally active and cannot entirely conceal his reactions from the outer world. You might need to master the craft of Sherlock Holmes and learn to analyse the most indirect of hints.

If your child is fearful of expressing his wishes in words, he will communicate them to you by writing on the wall, scratching the table, trampling the flowers in the garden, or some other destructive activity. It is on these occasions that you should show your child—and even more, yourself—that you love him. Your love will manifest in your readiness to try and understand the signals he's sending. Try to avoid your natural reactions. You might feel the urge to shout or hit him, but this will help nobody and only serve to increase the distance and estrangement between you. It is more important to ascertain the reasons for his protest.

Imagine that you are faced with a bed of trampled flowers. Adrenaline is racing through your veins and anger is roaring in your head. At moments like these, remember: your child is waiting for an answer from you, not a reaction. Try to understand that the offence you see is not the reality of the situation. You see the crushed flowers and recall all the hard work you put into tending to them; you remember how you were punished for similar offences as a child; you grouse about your child's ingratitude. All this heats up your emotions and you release that heat by deciding that he should be punished. Instead focus your thoughts not on the flowerbed and your horticultural labours, but on what is happening with your child. Ask yourself: why is he so angry with the world? Why is he not speaking to me? Where have I lost contact with him?

I once had a conversation with a woman who complained about her seven-year-old child. 'I had recently bought new furniture for my son's bedroom,' she said. 'I even bought an armchair with leather armrests. The next day I found that they had been ripped to shreds with a razor blade. Just imagine! What ingratitude! That was his reply to my hard work and love!'

I was interested to learn what had happened in her personal life just before she had made the purchases and it was just as I had expected: she had recently divorced her husband. Her son had interpreted the gift as a feeble attempt to compensate for the loss of his father. The swap was simply not enough, and the shredded armrests were intended to broadcast this message.

Parents, acting with the best of motives, sometimes make mistakes like this because they fail to attach proper significance to words or actions. The child's perception of the world is on a different scale. A child's nightmare may be a source of real fear for many months. A broken toy can assume the proportions of a tragedy. One of the mothers I once spoke with was talking about her memories of ten years before and she suddenly recognised the moment when she lost contact with her son. The boy, who was ten years old at the time, had saved up his pocket money for a birthday present for his best friend. His mother had given him extra money as well. The boy spent half a day deciding what to buy and finally chose a beautiful leather football but when the boy showed it to his mother and told her the price, she reacted, 'I wanted to save him from an embarrassing situation,' she said. 'I tried to explain to him that you can't give someone a present that costs the equivalent of his parents' monthly salary. My son tried to justify it, but I held firm to my point and he backed down and went to the party without a present. A month later I found the football in his wardrobe. He had cut it up with scissors.'

From that moment on, the mother and son were estranged from each other. The son stopped giving presents altogether, even simple gifts like flowers for her. The mother didn't understand and the boy could not explain his feelings coherently. 'My son was able to make sense of his anger and forgive me only when he had a son himself many years later and could see things from my perspective,' she said. The misunderstanding was cleared up, but only after ten years. How much time was wasted!

Something that might seem insignificant to adult understanding caused significant psychological barriers for this growing personality. This need not have happened if the mother had not been so insistent on protocol, and, more importantly, had tried to view the issue through the eyes of her son. If she could have given it more thought, it would not have been so difficult for her to find a compromise. This, in turn, could have opened the door to further and deeper communication.

5

Children Forge their Own Developmental Path

We have already noted the principal problem of raising children: that it is impossible to predict with precision the result of one influence or another. The same method can yield extremely diverse results. Interference on our part can evoke protest; asserting limits can evoke the urge to break them down. One person might develop more quickly if praised; another, if praised too much, might weaken and become dependent.

Parents, teachers, neighbours and playmates all play a part in moulding our personalities into a form acceptable to them, so the individual becomes human. This is called group identity. The child begins to judge and evaluate himself according to how the surrounding world relates to him.

Svyatoslav was three when his mother took him to see his grandmother in Moscow. He was there for a week. When he got back to Kitezh, he entered the house with a warm smile and a 'Hello, Papa!' It was nice, but something seemed to be missing. It wasn't quite the degree of excitement I expected after a big trip away from home. The next morning Svyatoslav counted off the names of members of the family—Mama, Papa, Sasha, Vasya, Kirill—instead of his usual 'Good Morning'. He went off to kindergarten with Nastya, the little girl with whom he had been so protective of his toys. Life settled back into its normal routine. Suddenly, three days later, as he put his toys down to go to bed, he looked around almost pensively and asked, 'Mama, is this my house? Is this Kitezh?' It had taken him three days to make sense of where he'd been; to process the differences between our home and Grandma's in Moscow.

Another novelty for him was the word 'my'. He started using it in connection with everything he could. 'I'm not giving Nastya my bike. It's mine. Don't touch my bed. That's my mama.' One particularly startling statement he uttered was, 'That's my real papa.'

Where had he heard that fathers could be real or not real? The adults at Kitezh don't talk about it and stress to the children that there is no difference between foster and real parents but there is a difference. The youngest children talk about it freely but the older children don't. Clearly they think about it but conceal their thoughts so as not to reveal their problems and vulnerability.

This is not a novel idea. The psychologist Erik Erickson distinguished stages of a child's development according to the extent of his independence from the expectations of society. The key here is stubbornness—the feeling that you are special in some way—and the continuity of the self, or ego. How do parents relate to this? The majority instinctively confuse their own self with that of their child. The inference is, what is good for me is good for my child. I was raised in this way. Revealed in this response is a common characteristic of human nature: the dependence on stereotypes in order to avoid, for the sake of economy, analysing the actual reality.

As a consequence, the child is given a foreign programme for self-realisation—one that doesn't necessarily fit. It is easy to forget that outside the home is the twenty-first century, and the world that is attempting to imprint itself on the consciousness of the child has little or nothing in common with the solid-as-a-rock stereotypes of the adult generation. Sometimes the effort to create a clone of oneself is grounded in the urge to compensate for one's own failures or disappointments, summed up in the attitude I'll give him everything I never got. Such a position prevents the parent from seeing objectively what is actually happening in the child's mind, the ambitions that are emerging in his consciousness—what he strives towards and what he shies away from.

In Kitezh we call this 'the semolina effect'. I recall how strongly I disliked semolina as a child, but my grandmother fed it to me all the same in the stubborn belief that it was good for me. Why did she think that? I suspect that in her childhood she also was forced to eat it for the same reason. Now I have my own children, and something in my consciousness insistently tells me to feed them the dreaded semolina. Why? Because that's how it's always been and what everyone does.

Parents who don't perceive the boundaries of their power over a child assume they have the right to inhibit or place boundaries on his character. They see before them not a personality in the early stages of formation, but a blank sheet of paper. This will inevitably lead to conflict—with, and within, the child.

Orphaned children who have been forced to survive by living on the streets have already been betrayed by life, regardless of their age. Children who have lost their parents can be tender or coarse, of gentle character or insolent, but they cannot be approached with the same standards or methods you may have developed through experience with your own children. There is something in them that is revealed only after many years and the process demands of you a very careful, professional and therapeutic approach.

Kitezh would fall under the Western definition of a 'therapeutic community' in that all of the interrelationships between foster parents, teachers and children are directed towards the rehabilitation and development of children who have been abandoned, and are without parental guardianship.

WHAT IS A 'NORMAL' CHILD?

We have already noted that each child comes into the world with a specific purpose, a programme of development, a prescribed path. As the American philosopher Abraham Maslow states, 'In the full sense of the word, the healthy personality can only be considered as a personality that is striving for growth.' A child whose development is uncorrupted is one who wants to discover everything himself. He becomes used to the world being safe and comfortable and to loving parents beside him whose help is as reliable as light and warmth. These developing personalities accept love as a given, believing that if others love them, that is because they deserve this love. This is the first stage of development: the child develops basic trust in the world. One of the first social achievements is when a child is willing to let his mother out of his sight without excessive anxiety or anger since her return is predictable and certain.

Erik Erickson, to whom we have already referred, calls the period up to the age of one (including the foetal stage) the period of formation of basic trust in the world. If all goes smoothly—if the child does not go unfed or is not left too long in his wet nappy, for example—then he will in all probability carry on for ten or twenty years in the comfortable belief that the world is an all-right place in which to romp around. With little or no exposure to real fear, he will grow up without insurmountable learning challenges and will get on with any project he undertakes. He will fall over and get up again, confident that falling over is a natural happenstance and will proceed with confidence and optimism. Of course, such an outlook can breed overconfidence and lead to countless problems. Absolute confidence in the world can be as dangerous as absolute pessimism. What is essential is moderation and balance, with a slight bias towards optimism and a willingness to take certain risks.

Every culture and historical period has its corresponding rules for the nursing of infants. Erickson writes (not without humour) that Russians have an unusually expressive stare because it is customary in Russia to carry a baby in one's arms so tightly wrapped in swaddling clothes that he can scarcely breathe, let alone cry. The only way he can attract the attention of his mother is to catch her eyes in a fixed and expressive gaze.

Between one to three years, the second stage of development where the child learns independence and autonomy, kicks in. Sometime around his third birthday my son Svyatoslav began to insist on his right to feed himself with a knife and fork, to open containers of food, to lay the table, and even to wash the dishes. We didn't stop him, but helped out in order to speed up the process. This would invariably be met with screams bordering on the hysterical and the repeated voicing of the words 'by myself!' He cried as he had never cried before, even when being scolded or falling over on the ground. 'By myself' became his words to live by, his motto for the very freedom for which adults will lay down their lives.

This 'I'll do it by myself', however, must have definite boundaries. When we went for a walk with Svyatoslav he would constantly ask, quite unexpectedly, 'Daddy, can you kill the wolf?' Only when he heard an affirmative answer would he let go of my hand and run off to explore the growth at the path's edge. Independence is inextricably connected with the confidence that one's parents are not far away and are always ready to lend support, whether it is physical or simply the ability to listen, sympathise, and praise. This is what a child at this age needs most of all. All of this can be summarised in one word: emotional support. It is the necessary prerequisite to independence and is the most important influence a parent can have over his or her child.

This fragile thread of support is snapped if the child is taken too early from his parents' guardianship—if he is taken to a nursery or a crèche before he is ready, if he is left alone for too long, or, in a far worse scenario, if drunkenness causes the parent to neglect his or her parental duty.

It can happen even in apparently 'good' families, albeit in a different form. The mother may want a baby so badly that she never leaves the side of the cradle, mollycoddling and smothering him with attention. The child perceives the mother's nervousness and learns to fear independence.

In less affluent families (especially in Russia in which alcohol abuse is extensive), frequent arguments and an indifferent attitude towards the child prevent the little one from concentrating on anything but basic survival. This corrupted development doesn't usually occur overnight, but the child doesn't progress normally into the first or second stage of development. He forms in his subconscious a view of the world as a dangerous and unpredictable place. In the second stage he is afraid of independence, as he can't know how his parents will react. Their reactions are unpredictable and inexplicable. He won't be able to understand when his parents praise and cuddle him or shout at or hit him, and he won't want to snuggle or display his feelings with anyone, lest they betray his trust. This fosters quite a different independent view of the world, and it is in this way that a passive type of personality develops. In practice the parents deprive their child of the possibility of fighting for his future and condemn him to a suffocating fear of self-expression.

A child who is paralysed by fear or excessively protective mothering will begin to lag behind in his development. As a rule, he will be aware of it; and because he cannot trust his own strength, he will seek the protection of others. Dependency helps him rid himself of his fear of independent choices.

The third stage of child development is imaginative play. This stage usually takes place between the ages of three and five and can be distinguished by active initiative and the child taking moral responsibility for his desires. The child characteristically will display the wish to be included in adult activity and to escape the role expected of him as a child. He should be encouraged to join in, not prevented from trying, and certainly not humiliated for any shortcomings or failures. One can warn him ahead of time that helping to clear up after a meal might end up with broken dishes—explain to him why hitting the cup against the bowl is not a good idea—but all the same, encourage his efforts. If you don't control your temper, he will begin to be frightened of trying new things or taking the initiative.

A normal child will rush excitedly towards anything that represents the outside world and will happily demonstrate his knowledge and experience. He derives satisfaction from this and he will try harder to impress. This becomes a cyclical developmental process, encouraged by the continuous pleasure in positive results. For a healthy child, the act of learning is encouragement in itself, if it results from his own choice and not at the insistence of his parents. Later the enthusiasm subsides, overtaken in adolescence by the need to understand one's place in the social order. In the meantime, the child should tend towards a positive understanding of the world. For you, your child's desire to expand his knowledge and accelerate his acquisition of new skills and talents should indicate that his intellectual health is developing normally. Always look upon it as an accomplishment, even when the process seems somehow to be directed against you.

Svyatoslav was two and a half when his mother decided to go away for a few days and leave me with the opportunity to get some practice at putting him to bed. He acted out a little bit, and I lost control and gave him a slap (inexcusable in all situations). He began crying and curled up, tucking himself in bed. I sat by him and was myself emotional as I listened to his sniffles. 'I'm going to go into the playroom,' he sniffed. 'I'm going to go, and then you'll miss me and you'll cry.' I remained silent, not sure how to respond to his just observation. Svyatoslav, wrongly interpreting my silence, dealt another blow: 'Mama doesn't love you, Papa. She loves me. And you'll cry.' I still didn't reply. I went to sleep that night calmly but carefully considering what had happened. Apparently my son could discern the finer elements of our mutual relationships. He knew that his mother loves both of us. He looked for and found my weak spot. He looked into my mind by looking into his own. He saw us as equals in our needs and feelings and rightly perceived that what is painful for him is painful for me too.

This means we have common values and that the path is open to mutual understanding. It seemed that Svyatoslav was able to identify himself with his parents, to look at the conflict afresh and, instead of his usual emotional reaction, find an appropriate mental response. I do not doubt that as he lay in bed he was plotting, 'When I grow up, I'll smack Papa too.' Healthy children have aspirations for the future; they are in a hurry to grow up and learn, see and experience as much as possible and earn responsibility and trust.

The term most often used for the process described here is 'self-initiated development', 'self-realisation', or 'self-knowledge'. Maslow considers these terms to be synonymous, in that they signify the ability to appreciate oneself and constantly develop one's abilities and to seek to realise one's ideas and hopes and to attain to greater understanding of what it is that makes up one's own identity.

Kitezh

DIFFICULT CHILDREN

The following is by Feodor (not his real name) orphaned at nine, given a home in Kitezh at fourteen and a law student at seventeen.

He writes:

During the years I have lived in Kitezh, I have been asked on several occasions to tell the story of my life. I have never really managed to do it. My foster father, Dimitry Morozov, explained to me that the reason he was pushing me to remember my past was to make the memories less painful. However, I felt after the third session during which I was telling my story that, in fact, it wasn't my story at all. It was like a picture on a wall. It's possible to look at it without crying. I'm not crying. But I thought that that subject had been over and done with a long time ago.

Now I'm a student in the law faculty of Kaluga University. I frequently return to Kitezh because it is my home. But it was not so before. I don't care what name you give to me. I even decided I would sign my own name, but then my teacher friends advised me against it, saying it might cause embarrassment in the future. So I'll call myself Feodor. It seems like a good name because it has something solid, fundamental, in tune with my character. I am writing my life story for the American specialists who have come to our therapeutic community because Dimitry asked me to.

[I spoke while he typed and I asked questions—some of them leading. So to some extent, it's our joint creation.]

Feodor: I was born eighteen years ago into a family of workers near the town of Kirov. At that time, when it was considered respectable to be a worker, there were many towns with that name. My town, the smallest of the Kirovs—so small, in fact, that it could only be seen on a map of the Kaluga region. I was the only child in my family and was born when my parents were already quite old. I never knew why.

During the first years, the idea never entered my head to ask why, and later there was simply no one to ask. In short, when I was born my mother was forty-two and my father was a few years younger. We lived in one room and were, as I now understand, poor. The only thing I remember from the earliest years is a May 1st demonstration. It was a clear day. There were balloons flying in the sky. I don't remember my parents being there but I do clearly remember how the arm they were holding me by went numb. I grew up really attached to home and hated going to Pioneer camps. Once I found that my mother had a pass for me to go to a Pioneer camp. Somehow she had got hold of a reduction for me and I shouted at her.

My father started to drink when I was in the second class, but I can't remember the first moment I noticed it. He often just lay on the couch, and I thought he was asleep. Then I started to hear Mama complaining about him. He would come home from work already drunk. He would be like that every day.

Maybe there was something wrong between him and my mother. I knew very little about his work and his life. It was rumoured that he had been in prison. He had a lot of tattoos. Maybe it was a habit, maybe bad memories. He was quite old. He was shorter than I am now. He had a dark complexion, black hair, with white curls. Damn! I don't remember him as being an old man.

They fought a lot but one day I came home from school and they were lying together, drunk. They could barely stand or walk. It's interesting how they could start off by arguing and then end up drinking together. People don't just argue with the people around them; they fight about their whole lives. At any particular moment, she would react to the person who seemed to be against her, even if that person is a husband or a son.

From that day on my mother drank every day. Sometimes she

was away from home for weeks. My father often couldn't walk after his drinking sessions and sent me to beg for money. He also had choking fits. When I was in the third class, I remember that Father started to choke, so my mother and I had to put a spoon in his throat so that he wouldn't choke to death.

It was a standard scenario: mother never at home; father lies at home and can only just say 'bring me something to eat'.

I had to go to the neighbours. It was really embarrassing. I was ashamed. I knew that in the other families the fathers worked and earned money on their own. The neighbours sometimes gave things, sometimes came and spoke with my father but he was always drunk and couldn't care less.

I very rarely studied; in fact, I hardly went to school at all. I have vague memories of how my class teacher would come to the house. But what could she say? She looked after me out of sheer kindness. I started to stay back with her after lessons and she helped me to do my homework, but then of course, I would run away.

I was born this way. I can understand anything that has to do with logic and once I understand it, I don't forget it. My inclination to observe appeared. If I liked to examine things so much, why is it so hard now to remember things? Hmmm. There is something else, though. My mother had a friend. There was some sort of conflict between the two women. Somebody had stolen a fur coat from someone else. I tried to listen to them, and at one point, I could hear them arguing in the next room: 'fur coat, fur coat'. It was clear that they'd had a fight, but then something else happened between them and my mother began to drink. She lost so many other friends.

I can only remember three words she said: 'I got mad!' I couldn't forget those words. I don't exactly remember which period of time it was but at one point we only had an old mattress on the floor, a couple of chairs, a gas fire and a TV left in the flat. If I remember correctly, my mother even sold my jeans in order to drink. I am remembering moments like that now whereas I never remembered them before.

I can't even say exactly how old I was when my mother was murdered. I can't remember. I was probably about nine. The weird thing is, I can't even remember it being a big deal at the time. It didn't make much difference whether she was there or not. There was just one thing that bothered me: why were they so cruel to her?

Dimitry: And how did your father react to the death of your mother?

Feodor: He stopped drinking. He stopped for a long time, by his standards. He was really shocked by her death; he tried to do something, to work for a tiny amount of money. He kept it up for a month; he tried to start a new life. He was pathetic, stooped. To make a long story short, he managed for about a month and then was thrown out of his job. Maybe he had stolen something. And then it all started again. At that time, Father told me to start going back to school again. I had missed a lot by then but the whole class looked at me as if I were a tramp and didn't accept me. Rumours spread quickly.

Dimitry: Did you have any friends?

Feodor: I did, but there were times when they hid from me. Naturally, it was impossible to study. When my father began to drink again, I went to get my mother's brother. At this moment I was very afraid. Father was lying on his side, groaning. I pretended that I was worried about his health. In reality, I couldn't bring myself to tell them straight away about his drinking. My father was totally out of it. My uncle came and saw everything, and decided to appeal to the social services. I had such hopes that my uncle would be able to force Father to look after me. I had the impression that he was clever and authoritative.

I looked for food; I had plans to work in the factory to be able to support my father. I felt sorry for him. What could I do with him? But the orphanage stopped everything. They arrived and forced my father to give up his parental rights. Then there began a strange period when I was moved from one orphanage to another. I can't actually remember how many of them there were. Each school had its own curriculum. It would have taken more time, and I would have had to get used to the classes. I was always the 'the new one', an outsider. They all knew I was from the orphanage. Anyway, that's what I'm guessing now but at the time I didn't realise what was so peculiar about me. It was just awful. Just like a crazy dream.

As soon as I arrived and settled down, a car would arrive and I would gather my things together. Where are they carting me off to? Why are they taking me? Now I don't have any emotional reaction when I bring to mind these memories, but I just can't fill the gaps in the memory loss. A car would appear from nowhere and take me to a new orphanage. There was one time when some people arrived from somewhere or other and said that my distant relatives were from Uzbekistan. They took me to Kirov. They had a flat where I stayed. I can't really remember them or the flat, either. I stayed there for a month. I even started at a school. Not long ago when I went back to Kirov, I tried to remember where the flat and the school were, but I couldn't find them. They weren't bad people; they told me that when I finished school we would travel to Uzbekistan. They said there were big watermelons there. But I never got to see the watermelons. When they realised that I wasn't capable of studying and that it was impossible to force me to do my homework, they sent me back to the orphanage. I don't know whose initiative that was—maybe someone from the social department.

At that time I imagined that an evil woman with her hair in a tight bun and glasses on her nose was constantly moving my papers from one table to another, which meant I would be moved from one place to another similar place. I was going slightly mad from seeing all these places that looked the same. Then I got lucky. I was sent to a small orphanage in Kirov and wasn't moved. Damn, I can't remember how I got there. I wonder why I can't remember anything about that period, difficult to believe, but I really can't remember. At that orphanage I made some friends, I started to study, and all the pupils in my class had parties. Another girl and I even visited Denmark.

This last period of Feodor's life was already known to us. He really was lucky: this small orphanage (thirty children) outside Kirov had an excellent director and supervisor. They really looked after their children and cultivated a positive collective atmosphere of openness, cooperation and trust where the children's needs were concerned. They sent Feodor to Kaluga to take part in a physics/maths competition to which he had been invited by the teachers of the physics/maths correspondence school. He won the prize of a two-week holiday in Kitezh for an intensive development course.

Feodor: Well, you know, even the psychologists at the orphanage would look at my drawings—'Look at the big eyes: it means he's frightened of something'. I did it on purpose so that I would be noticed. I was the oldest on my floor. They made me responsible for the cleaning. I wanted, as I remember now, to combine two things: to be a leader and to be invisible. I know it seems strange, but I was always strange to others. I saw graphs, thought about them, and realised it was possible to draw the curves of the formulas. Each has its own formula, so it's possible to give the formula to a machine and the machine works it out. That's how the teacher explained how functions relate to the graphs. If I do like something, I look for the logic and then it's easy for me. I liked geometry, and I debated it with the teacher. She wanted me to learn the theorems, but everything was clear to me from the drawings. I didn't want to recite the theorems because I already knew the right answers.

Dimitry: And how did you feel in Kitezh? What seemed more important—a foster family or what we call a community?

Feodor: I didn't recognise the community, as such. The family was enough, and it was difficult. The first days I did as much as I could. I played on the computer and rode on the horse. Then, when I realised that I didn't have much time left, I started to look at the people who were around me. I saw them as if through opaque glass. Probably, by that time, I had already forgotten what a real family was. I had gotten used to friends and matrons.

I probably understood that when I liked a place, I considered it to be my home. I didn't want to leave Kitezh. You had such a different atmosphere in your community. No one was putting pressure on anyone. Teachers were merry and helped the children to learn. I liked English and maths, but I was confrontational. I wasn't used to socialising. I never had any parental support. Before then, I hardly had any friends. Some sort of bad incident, maybe during childhood, stopped me from wanting to get to know myself. I thought about anything I wanted to as long as it wasn't about myself. I had two worlds before then: orphanage and the big world. I hadn't imagined what there would be after the orphanage. I told myself that sooner or later something had to happen and I didn't worry about it. That's how it was in Kitezh for the first years.

Dimitry: Why did you reject your first foster family in Kitezh?

Feodor: I don't know. [He is emotional, with a false smile.] Why don't I know that? It's my own life, damn it!

Dimitry: And now, do you understand why you don't remember?

Feodor: Because I don't want to remember. I wasn't really comfortable there with my new foster parents but I just knew that the orphanage would get on my nerves even more. I never felt that it was my real family. I remembered what my real family was: my dead mother and my father with no parental rights. I understood that it would be better not to show it to my new one but I understood that they did a lot for me; they fed me. I managed to avoid being at home too often. I hung out in other Kitezh houses, where there wasn't a regime (rota) for doing the washing up. Then a psychologist came to visit. His name was Stepan and he spoke to my foster parents. They listened to him and began to speak more openly and from the heart. They changed the way they treated me. But I understood that they were only doing what the psychologist told them to do. I liked him a lot myself. We philosophised…he explained psychological things to me. It was easy to talk to him about anything. He probably heard everything I couldn't say to my foster parents. I didn't believe them.

Dimitry: But why did you believe him?

Feodor: I don't know. He seemed to be free, in his own way, I think. I wanted to be like him.

[He was fat, lazy and untidy. What's more, he smelt of foul tobacco, sweated, wore glasses and had a straggly beard. You could see that half his teeth were missing. And Stepan, who had finished a crash course in commerce organised by an American firm, wasn't a professional psychologist in the full sense but he had the time and inclination to talk to people about their inner world. Clearly he was the first person Feodor had ever met to whom he felt he could speak about any topic. It is interesting that Feodor's foster father also spent long hours talking to Stepan.]

Feodor: It was fun with Stepan; he made jokes and was popular with all the other lads.

Dimitry: And he used to smoke like a chimney in your presence.

Feodor: He said it wasn't really such a bad thing. I can't really remember what we used to talk about—a bit of everything, I suppose.

Dimitry: I assume he wasn't a threat to you because he was far from ideal himself. You compared yourself with him and even felt superior to him and this allowed you to absorb knowledge without feeling threatened. With me it was impossible for you to relax. You thought I wanted more from you than you could give. But with Stepan everything fell into place.

Feodor: You're right. I now think that I didn't want to be like him at all but at the time I failed to understand that.

Dimitry: Let's take another look at the problems with your foster parents.

Feodor: We were just different. I refused to keep to schedules and structures. I'm not used to reading books when others want me to. My foster father said that I should spend more time at home and talk to him for an hour every day. He also had a very strange little book about professions and the laws governing the structure of society. He told me very interesting things about it.

It's easier to take such things from friends than from adults. Now that we have a mentor system, we've learned to deal with these conflicts. But at that time who was there to tell me? I told my friends that I loathed my foster family and nobody told me I was wrong. They just avoided the subject. Perhaps they couldn't handle problems like that.

From these negative emotional experiences grew the morbid idea, as I told you, about becoming a pathologist—probably because I wanted to look cool. There's something nihilistic about dissecting bodies.

Probably it had something to do with my rapport with my

first foster father. I've already told you that we talked to each other every day. He told me how I should behave. His 'lectures' bore no relation to what I personally wanted. I felt small and defenceless up against him, but I didn't want to be like him. I've only just realised that in other respects everything in my life was as it should be. But just that one little thing would have been enough to drive me out of my foster family.

A child's awareness is plastic and all embracing. If you expose him not to the real world but to a sham, a brightly coloured façade, he will soon see through it and will never trust you again. Personal experience of life is of greater use than a teacher's guidance. This means that the world in which the child develops should be real, soundly based, have integrity, and therefore facilitate the child's quest for perception, strength and love.

The inconsistencies that are peculiar to adult life should not, at the therapy stage, cloud the general picture. As the experience of Kitezh shows, by acquiring knowledge and confidence, children are then adequately equipped to face the difficulties of adult life. In order to grow up, however, and gather strength and experience, they must first of all be provided with the right conditions. The first of these is the integrity of adults and their unshakable belief in the values they inculcate.

Foster Family A had to leave the therapeutic community and the children were given the choice of whether to stay in Kitezh or leave with their foster parents. All the children chose to stay in Kitezh. It stands to reason that such extreme situations are very rare and the majority of adult helpers in Kitezh are devoted to their children and understand how essential it is to work hand in hand with the pedagogical counsel so as to create a unified developing environment.

Feodor: I didn't suffer when my foster parents went away, I

just didn't feel anything. In the Terentev family, where you sent me for a while, you didn't have to wash the floor on a regular and mandatory basis; there was much more freedom and you could adopt a 'couldn't-care-less' attitude.

As I now understand, if the world doesn't affect you, then you put it to one side but if it does affect you, you begin to reckon with it. I understand we now call this a 'challenge'. Yes, I now realise how great it is that you can go up to different adults and talk to each of them. At the time Marina, one of the Kitezh teachers, was particularly helpful. For two weeks she patiently got me to consider just one thing: how you shouldn't be afraid of yourself.

And that trip boosted my self-esteem. Of course at that time I wasn't able to make any appraisal of Kitezh because I wasn't part of the place but I felt I had changed. I remember a serious conversation took place in the car. It was hard both to speak and to listen. But I didn't realise at the time that this was because of the pressure. I wasn't fully aware of it at the time, but another stage was coming to an end. I decided to join you.

Well, of course, I heard and understood what you had to say, but I didn't go any further. I couldn't. The main thing I felt was a wave of energy, a positive attitude. They were going somewhere, driving the car on my behalf. And the greatest thing to come out of it was that I ended up in a family—this time in yours.

I waited until school ended and I was off to the Army. But I didn't want to go. I realised that if I didn't start maturing, strike up a rapport with the teachers, and even make compromises, then I'd end up there. Around that time Pasha, Alexandra and Masha had turned up in Kitezh and they had no trouble relating to adults. And the good thing was I wasn't alone. Pasha and I had become friends; he was the one who actually got me into your house. These three respected you but weren't afraid of you. I realised this and wanted to follow their example. I also saw that Morozov is not the disapproving uncle with the long beard who keeps you on the alert the whole time. You don't allow people to be absorbed with routine, but I initially thought this was something negative. Now I understand it leads to awareness.

I often realise I've changed. But there wasn't really one moment when I actually opened up. When the process is ongoing, you don't notice it.

You personally tried to get me interested: first of all, with history lessons and your attitude towards me. But the family itself had some tension about it. It was all rather unusual.

You managed to get through to me when you brought up the idea of 'unfairness'. I realised I'd been unfair to you. Sometimes the thought crossed my mind, but there was never any substance to it. I needed help for it to sink in.

I suddenly realised I was treating you unfairly. I decided to try, to attempt to change something. I'd begun to do something and I had less of a sense of doom. Until then I'd gone around with my head held low and I'd filled it with all sorts of nonsense, but now I knew where to go. I just thought, is there a way of achieving this painlessly?

I'm grateful now. What difference does it make if you extract a tooth without an injection; in the end it no longer hurts? I gradually realised what you were drumming into me. Each conversation with you helped us take things further. You persuaded me to try to act; you clarified the picture. You had the feeling it was a sort of journey. It was interesting that the conversation could be about any topic; whatever it was, it inspired confidence, just as the conversations in our circle of older children, even without adults, also inspire confidence.

From December 2000 to May 2001 the following changes took place: Feodor found confidence in himself, became an avid reader, took care of his appearance and clothes, and agreed to become a member of the children's Small Counsel, even though he doesn't like being a high-profile leader or taking on responsibility. He was, nevertheless, elected leader of the Small Council, he studies well, and dreams of becoming a lawyer and studying in Moscow. In his languid and spiritual moments he writes poetry and sings. He is interested in psychology and tries to control his feelings. He has something approaching love for his foster parents—at least they love him and take pride in his success.

Feodor: I was impressed by what Khlopenov, the community leader, said at one of the meetings: 'Kitezh is the road that I follow.' Then I realised there was nowhere else I could go—it really was my 'road'. Not in the sense that I stay here because there's nowhere else to hide. Simply by living my life here I can feel joy. I thought up the following aphorism for myself: 'From two pleasures you must choose the one that is useful to you'. When I started studying in Kaluga, I thought that in the first few weeks I wouldn't make it. This became my one big problem— being away from Kitezh and doing nothing for Kitezh. The thought entered my head that you can't just be afraid and do nothing about it. I realised I'm working for the future. Once I've finished my studies, I'll be able to help more. That's it. I've got no more to add, because I know when I wake up at night, I'll start to worry that I didn't actually say that, or I left out something important. Let's leave it as it is.

That is the end for the time being, but Feodor's story goes on as his life does and there are still many challenges for him. What was a greater surprise for us is that trauma experienced in early childhood influenced the whole life for many years, and that by moving a child from the street or an orphanage to better surroundings does not necessarily change his inner image of the world.

Children who lose their parents also lose their intuitive feeling for the route to self-realisation, as well as qualities that are necessary for continuing their development. Difficult children get into trouble because they have lost touch with the path to an independent, self-realised future. What do we adults do when we are lost? We turn around and go back until we find another path or look for someone from whom we can request help.

Here we encounter the great chasm between children whose development is normal in the early stages and those who have at some point survived a personal tragedy, been deprived of parental support, have been abandoned, or have lived in fear of being beaten. Children who have had a normal development might live in blissful ignorance of the dangers of the world and can more easily progress in life, study, dare to do new and different things, and enjoy the thrills and surprises of life. Deprived children quickly learn that nobody is around to look after them and that they will have to get along by themselves. They will be afraid to play and explore freely because of their uncertainty of where the boundary of danger lies.

Let us remember that an extended period of separation from one's parents or an excessively powerful combination of overly strict control, violence and conflict in the family can stop, slow down, or distort a child's development. A child can end up feeling strong resentment at the world, anger at the person who he feels has abandoned him, and lack of belief in his own strengths. When traumatic experiences are severe or prolonged, they act like a virus, leaving a wound in the very core of his being. Whatever experience child has later it will encounter this residual virus. Everything will be filtered through his entrenched conception of the injustice and danger of the world.

Our main task, then, is to change this programme for processing information. Nature, however, has hidden the 'programme discs' so deeply that no programmer can access them without the risk of breaking the whole personality. (I use this computer analogy only as an illustration. Heaven forbid that anyone would seriously equate a child with a computer.) The famed Hindu ascetic Sri Ramakrishna often repeated this parable: 'A potter crafts pots from soft clay: if he doesn't like one, he can crumple it up and start again, but once he has baked the pot, then it is too late to remake it. He can only smash it…'

Children who have lived through a family crisis are burned by life, and it becomes extremely difficult then to change their worldview. That does not mean to say, however, that it is impossible.

In the first years of our work at Kitezh we were touched by the scene of foster parents dashing about at work with their children closely in tow. Only with time did we realise that the child's tendency to cling suggested anxiety and the attempt to control his own safety. In such a situation, you—the parent—must accustom your child to the fact that you will always return and that he will never lose you. Until both of you have passed this stage, the child will never be rid of his innate anxiety which will in turn not allow his normal self-initiated development. As Maslow wrote, 'Children prefer not to see reality as it scares them.'

A child is taken into a family. He is washed, clothed and fed; he smiles; he even helps with housekeeping and does his homework. His personal problems are locked away deep inside; they are his hidden secret, which he feels he must not reveal to anyone. He might rationalise: 'I must be bad because my parents left me. My memories are horrible so I'm going to forget about it and never think about it. Nobody can love me, so there's no point in trying to make friends or trusting anyone.'

Many children at Kitezh experienced in the early stages of their lives such injustices and grief that subconsciously they learned to expect more of the same for the rest of their life. The adults at Kitezh don't try to persuade them to the contrary because an individual with such strong convictions is convinced otherwise only by experience. Whatever is contrary to his experience is merely a fairy tale.

Biological children soak up their family's values as if they were their mother's milk. They might eventually reject them, but they reject them as something to which they had grown accustomed, something familiar that they eventually find boring. Fostered children do not take on the values of their new parents, for quite a different reason. Even if they are in an ideal family and are exposed to positive examples from strong and happy adults, they are prone to continue embracing their own validity. Their moral values are muddled and they are unaccustomed to joy, and because of this they are not easily persuaded to follow their foster parents' example. In order truly to appreciate the world's goodness and beauty, one needs to open one's eyes and this is precisely what the damaged child's instinct for self-protection doesn't allow.

Andrei is twelve years old: 'I'm never rude. I'm like a mouse: I might play a trick on you and then run away. I think I'm open and honest.'

You can make a compromise with him, find a middle way, and sustain harmony in the family. Then the shell remains a shell and protects the inner, vulnerable person from the realities of the world while stunting his growth and development. This manifests itself most obviously at school, where certain qualities are required, such as decisiveness, the readiness to build relationships with his surroundings, the motivation to do homework, and the willingness to join in cultural activities. Where is he to get the strength of will to achieve this if not from his inner world? But that has been cut off as forbidden territory, the realm of demons from the past. Facing one's problems honestly can be intolerable and many prefer to hide from them. One of the most vital roles of foster parents is to help their children make peace with their past so that they can move forward with their personal development.

The biblical parable about talents might be considered applicable to the plight of Kitezh's children. The parable's moral is that it is sinful to bury ones talents in the ground, to deny one's divinely given chances of development. 'We wish any person that which is highest, most light, and most joyful. We do not wish him a greater quantity of dull, petty joys; we desire that he should grow in such proportions that his joy will be great, that he will enjoy fullness of life... May his life be as full and beautiful as is possible.'

This same idea was expressed in different words, by Abraham Maslow. Without transcending the bounds of scientific research, he showed that a normal person seeks self-realisation. According to Maslow, 'a person's aspiration is to become everything that he is capable of becoming, to fully realise his potential.'

6

The Developing Environment

Phillip is a difficult child. He has learned to read and count, but at six years old, he still does everything his parents tell him not to: breaks toys, squirms to avoid doing his homework and so forth. At the stage when Phillip was learning to recognise the world and gain impressions of the interactions around him, his parents were serious drinkers. His mind learned and his body hardened to the truth that the world is based on violence and pain and that the only way to survive is to steal, avoid attention, attack first and always blame someone else.

As long as Phillip was able to verify his view of the world through his experiences, he was able to relax. He did not reflect on his problems, did not retain new experiences in his memory, and did not register the limits and rules by which others lived. He was very careful, however, to ensure that his personal understanding of what was right and just was not violated. Because of this, wherever Phillip went he got into fights and arguments. Of course, the laws of interaction, which he did not recognise, nevertheless functioned. Phillip was punished; his peers shouted at him, the girls avoided him, yet he remained certain that these were problems in the reality surrounding him. He could not see any problem in his own behaviour, because according to the laws of survival in the wild (or in a family of alcoholics living outside society's laws), he had no other choice if he wanted to survive. He was punished over and over again, and still did not change. We approached him gently and with affection, as we should, but he did not respond.

What would persuade you that your experience was not true if you had been beaten as a child? Only one thing: a profound recognition that everything was a lie. You weren't beaten up. That wasn't your experience! That's not your world! The main role of therapy is to bring these internal obstacles to the surface so they can be seen for what they are. This can only happen with external support.

Many people growing up in the 1970s will have read Alfred Bester's classic novel *The Demolished Man*. In this society of the future, criminals are not punished. They are treated. Ben Reich, a millionaire, commits a murder. With the help of telepathic parapsychologists called 'Espères', he sets up a virtual world in his head, where he is convinced he lives (the Hindus called this maia). He continues to think, feel and act without recognising that instead of inhabiting the real world he has sunk into a virtual world. He is surprised, therefore, when he finds large contradictions between his lifelong notions of the world and that which he now perceives as reality. For example, in this new reality there are no stars and no Paris; even the Espères and his own business do not exist.

Reich, who relies on his physical senses, cannot doubt the reality of the world he sees. The new picture of the world completely erases the old one from his memory. Everything that had meaning until that point was destroyed, as if crushed under the pressure of the new, incontrovertible reality. This is referred to in the novel as the 'demolition'. Later, the doctors reconstruct a personality for Riech that works from a basis of good.

With Phillip, we had constantly to compel him to recognise

that he was behaving wrongly when he made mistakes in relating to other people. He did not make mistakes in relating to the world of nature—he did not bang his head against trees, was perfectly happy on a bike, was better than most at looking for mushrooms and was mad about acrobatics. Problems arose only with other people. The Teachers' Council, which is also attended by peer mentors, concluded that we needed to show Phillip that the world of people is distinguishable from the world of nature.

We exerted gentle yet powerful pressure to dissuade Phillip from reacting automatically to his surroundings. We subjected every coarse word to judgment and every outburst of emotion to analysis. We literally forced him to analyse his movements and interactions with his surroundings.

Within a period of time, the community's collective effort had completely changed the world surrounding Phillip. It became a stable world where any expression of aggression was responded to severely and where people would not submit to his usual behaviour. Phillip could no longer get angry with individuals; he was no longer struggling against individuals but the community itself. In order to survive in these new conditions, he had to restructure his programme of behaviour, to seek advice from the adults he trusted about how to change himself.

Then one day, as we were analysing one of his attacks on a peer, he suddenly exclaimed, 'Look I'm trying!' Like a Zen master in a medieval Japanese monastery, I was suddenly struck by a moment of realisation: he had indeed started to try. The goal of our therapy had been achieved. The rest would come with time as his newly awakened habit of recognising his conduct and emotions strengthened with the help of the community.

A child's internal programme for development functions against the backdrop of his living conditions from which he freely, if unpredictably, takes in information and experiences. We cannot influence the internal programme, but it is certainly within our power to make his surroundings as dynamic as possible and such as will stimulate his development.

We call living conditions at Kitezh a 'developing environment' because they are shaped by our interest in the accelerated development of children. Such an approach to upbringing demands deeply responsible, thoughtful behaviour from the adults. In the tradition of humanistic pedagogy we assume that adults will not only teach their children but will open up the world to them, help them understand themselves, recognise their mistakes and develop their talents and skills.

It is essential to create a special developing environment for children with psychological problems, one that helps them develop in accordance with their instincts and compensates for their problems and shortcomings. As we use the term, 'developing environment' refers to more than the special games, posters and puzzles found in nursery school. Those who have the greatest influence on a child are his parents, teachers and friends and together they form the basis of a developing environment.

A child's world consists not only of his social circle but also of material elements. By 'environment' we mean the natural world, as well as the material, spiritual and cultural influences and that can reinforce or negate parental influences. For example, inspirational poetry aids development while coarse rap lyrics hinder it.

The child retains his right to make choices but the choices he can make are not unlimited. In the developing environment at Kitezh, everything that is genuinely dangerous or bad is eliminated from the child's life. He cannot choose not to read, but he can choose the particular book he wants to read. He cannot choose not to work, but he can choose the type of work that best suits him. This freedom of choice within limits gradually gives rise to new aspirations and desires and engenders profound change in the child. This is achieved by setting up real-life situations rather than by lecturing him and giving orders. Each time a child is faced with a life challenge, he has the chance to overcome his personal weaknesses, strengthen his abilities, and increase his knowledge. His adult mentors make sure that the challenge before him is not beyond his capacities, and they help him to think creatively about what should be done, thus encouraging independent problem-solving.

Children learn from adults—or rather, they examine the view of the world presented by adults, testing it for 'lifelikeness' and integrity by comparing it against that which they know to be true. If the same view of the world is held by all of the adults in a child's life and if this view is consistent and clear, then the child will simply accept it, testing it from time to time for durability and veracity. It is of paramount importance, therefore, that Kitezh's adults do not express contradictory views to the child and that they personally believe in the values they are teaching. If children hear one thing in the classroom and something different at home (through their parents' bedroom wall, for example), they will simply refuse to accept the values put forth by the adults and will start to create their own subculture.

The Kitezh developing environment consists of three elements:

1. The foster family, which gives the homeless child that which is most important: the sense that he is needed and loved. This perception is essential if the child is to develop properly.

2. The community of competent adults, which provides the child with a safe environment in which he can develop the ability to live and work as part of a collective and which recognises the right of each and every person to their own individuality.

3. The natural environment and the architecture, which benefit the child spiritually, guides him to look for beauty and

harmony, reduces psychological distress, and provides surroundings that are conducive to therapeutic work.

Communication between an adult and a child is a creative process based on love and inspiration. Raising a child is an art that is impossible without love, compassion and inspiration. Only then can professionalism play its positive role. No foster parent can manage without both.

By describing the methods our foster parents and therapists use, we have attempted to clarify the laws governing the development of our social environment. This environment has been artificially created and has been shaped by the input of several of the foster families while remaining rooted in the reality of contemporary Russia. One cannot understand what is going on in Kitezh without analysing the four sectors of everyday life that constitute the integral whole:

The potential of every individual person.

The dynamics within each family.

The interaction between the families within the community.

The links between the community as an integral organism and the outside world.

The top priority in this pyramid of values must be the well-being of the orphaned child because it was for his development that the community was created in the first place.

Included in this experiment are many features that are exclusive to the Russian experience of life. Europeans with their love of logical analysis and structure may find them controversial, but the ways of any society can, and often do, contradict those in different parts of the world.

In ancient Russia, or Rus, the traditional peasant community was called the *mir* (in Russian, this word has two meanings: the world and peace). It was based on the most simple and eternal human interactions: mutual assistance, the ability to share, and the raising of children collectively. Every community demanded of its inhabitants responsible behaviour, participation in leadership functions, and willingness to work for the common good. To reflect this historical tradition, we decided to call our *mir* a community, *obshina*—a word that in Russian has stronger cultural and traditional connotations than in English. The Russian word *obshina* clearly expresses togetherness; our effort to create a life together, to solve problems together, and to make decisions together. The need to work together to survive has been a distinctive but not uniquely Russian problem.

We are attempting to live off the land and to love and value the land we live on. We are planning our own agricultural programme, but this does not stop our children from sinking their teeth into modern science and technology, from publishing their own newspaper on the Web, or engaging in other activities such as performing in theatre productions and dance shows, doing martial arts, or going on canoe trips. Among the adults of Kitezh, we have a former international correspondent, a former nuclear submarine engineer, an icon painter, a doctor and a computer programmer, to name a few. This diverse group of people is united by the common desire to help children and to live in harmony with each other and the environment.

CHALLENGES

The British educational innovator, David Dean, who founded a school for traumatised children, once said that he envies me because in Kitezh we have the freedom to throw genuine obstacles at our children. At first I didn't understand what he meant and asked him to explain:

I am now not confident that we have the freedom to allow children to chop wood for the school's wood stoves, or perhaps I would allow two boys each day to chop wood outside my window so that I could personally supervise them and be sure of their safety. We are also warned against the physical comforting of children as this could be interpreted as illicit sexual attention. Even being alone with a child in a room can be looked on by colleagues with suspicion; such is the climate of sanitised childcare we are experiencing in the UK currently. The whole area of the physical restraint of young people who are endangering others, themselves or property remains an absolute minefield despite several attempts by authorities and experts to define the parameters.

I would say that such a society has chased after safety to the point of utter paranoia. It sounds like a heaven for bureaucrats and lawyers but a hell for teachers. Everything has to be under somebody's control but what about the needs of the children? Where are they going to learn to chop wood, or any life skills which entail some element of risk? Surely, beyond the safe boundaries of the boarding school or foster family, in the big wide world that the children eventually are released into, life is full of real problems and dangers. Don't children need to learn to develop the skills to face them? I suppose this doesn't concern the bureaucrats and legislators. To them what is important is safety, creating empty lives deprived of risk and robbed of the chance for self-realisation.

We are deeply convinced that children should be able to chop wood and not be afraid of being alone with adults, who should not only be allowed but encouraged to touch and hug children, as physical contact is key to a child's personal development. Only through challenges can the child gain experience and develop the qualities lying dormant within him. Would we have great works of art if their creators had not suffered for their inspiration?

In Kitezh, each child is given the opportunity to try out the world at his own pace. The little ones are given responsibility for cleaning the house and helping in the kitchen and vegetable garden. The older children look after the little ones, taking them to lessons and organising collective activities and games.

All the information about the children's activities flows back to the Teachers' Council, and their accomplishments and shortcomings are passed on to their parents, who are then expected to praise them or give them a nudge as needed. This openness and coordination among the adults provides an additional opportunity to support the children in making positive changes and to express happiness with their discoveries and banish their doubts. Thus it is difficult for them to manipulate the adults and hide their activities from them. Of course, children—especially emotionally damaged children—can progress and regress at the same time, so we don't expect that the process will always be smooth and linear. We would hope, however, that all children, whatever their ages and the crises they have been through, are on their way to independence, responsibility and the expansion of their capabilities.

ADULTS IN KITEZH

We seek to manifest in Kitezh a common conviction in the truth and integrity of the values we teach, thus producing an inner harmony and agreement among the adults. These are based in a general way on humanitarian values and are the result of a consensual, democratic process. This does give community members a licence to say whatever comes into their heads or to violate their commitment when it suits their purposes. Common vision is incompatible with anarchy. The community has developed and become subject to certain internal laws.

The stumbling block for many people in a community is the need for a common vision. As mentioned above, in our therapeutic community we ask all the adults to adhere to values, which can be described as democratic and humanitarian. Kitezh is a therapeutic community, a place where people receive treatment. Kitezh residents must therefore recognise a certain limit to their individual freedom. Children receive treatment at Kitezh for emotional problems and this is not always evident to non-professionals. To bring up children whose entire value system has already imploded once and who need a holistic, reliable, consistent and safe world, it is essential that all the adults observe certain principles in their interactions with others. Even after all these years as a community, the answers to two questions still elude us: What do we want our children to be like once they are raised, and what are we building in Kitezh?

Building a social organism is in no way similar to building a car or a house. People have free will and the ability to develop. They don't want to fulfill the same function year in and year out; rather, they aim to fulfill their own ambitions. Any entrepreneur who has hired staff and assigned roles and responsibilities has been confronted by the awkward wilfulness in humans. The life of someone who lives in a community, however, cannot be reduced to a distinct job description. Our members' roles cannot be boiled down exclusively to teacher or foster parent. It would not be wise to regulate their activities strictly if it meant forsaking the chance to improvise and develop emotional connections between the children and foster parents. How would one write as a job description, 'empathise with tears in your eyes' or 'make room for them in your heart' or 'share thoughts with your children' all at the same time? Not the same as, 'fill out the questionnaires' or 'compare income and expenses'.

The above make sense if you understand that you are

encouraging a person to grow rather than programming a robot. Robots need an authoritarian power that hides its lack of personality behind bureaucratic slogans about 'nurturing specialists to enhance society and the economy'. We think that each and every person ought to be able to discover for himself the whole spectrum of innate talent within him and fully realise his potential. Solving economic and social challenges may be important, but is perhaps a secondary priority.

In the picture of the community, it is the people who fill in the colours with their hopes, character, ambitions and dreams. They are creating a new world, which in the moment of creation is unstable, naïve, and emotionally unbalanced. Our dreams are not generally strengthened by life's experiences. Typically, idealists who dream of a new world have difficulty getting by in the present one.

The history of our country and the world reveals that abstract, scientific constructions have one fatal flaw: they don't stand up to the test of life. Our community is constantly changing. That alone is proof that it stands the test of time and responds to the laws of social development.

When I planned Kitezh, I thought that the community's organisational structure would respond to the task of creating a united teaching collective. It was an enticing idea: everyone working and resting together and owning the property communally. There would be no competition or conflicts. My view of an ideal community was a collection of consciously well-educated people working together. Many people, unfortunately, perceive a community either as some variation on the ancient village of Rus, where land was redistributed regularly, or as some sort of cross between a religious sect and a prototype of a Communist collective. Now I wonder if it was worth trying to adopt administrative systems to provide stability and enclosure. A protective shell might preserve the status quo but it is also an obstacle to new sources of energy and deprives those inside of the chance of making evolutionary choices.

Kitezh is above all a therapeutic community. Here people don't live together as much as they work together. We have learned that it is a therapeutic community for all as no adult is immune from their own personal demons. The adults need to work on themselves in order to create a developing environment for children who have lost parental guardianship and have been abandoned in crisis situations. This work is the backbone of our existence as well as a vocation.

Objectivity is not one of the essential virtues of a foster parent. Only by intensely feeling empathy and by sharing children's fortunes and troubles can a foster parent or teacher in a therapeutic community identify with them and get a clear picture of their inner world. Intuition is as important for a teacher as it is for an artist. The objective is to attain an inner peace, which opens the door to empathy, or identification with others. One word for this process that is used in Waldorf schools is meditation. Meditation comes from the Latin word meaning contemplation. The term is often associated with Eastern religion, and tends to be used inaccurately because it covers several completely different methods a person can employ to immerse himself in his thoughts and emotions. The ability to relax and concentrate lowers and stabilises a person's emotional peaks and troughs, helping him to overcome fear and escape from external irritations. It introduces harmony into his thoughts.

The art of raising children is a state of permanent awareness. A child might ask you a question at any moment, or he could be listening to or watching what you're doing. At any moment, he could become sick or discouraged. Parents don't get weekends off or lunch breaks; they don't have any personal space in which they are free to forget the children. Parents might visit friends or go away on business, but they must remain aware of their children: who is caring for them? If the parents are absent and their children are watching television, another adult must be present, perhaps discussing the film or noting the children's reactions.

A therapeutic community is a place for healing. Nobody in a hospital is bothered by the requirement of having to observe hygienic practices or by the prohibition against stroke patients playing football. It's simply accepted. Certain situations in life mandate some restrictions on adults' personal freedom. Responsible parents become aware of this with the arrival of their natural children; in a therapeutic community, it is a conscious decision. When we created a therapeutic community, we took upon ourselves the responsibility of creating a safe developing environment for the children living with us.

There are many modern theories about how children 'should' change. We would say that a person who works with children (a psychologist, for example) should always remember that he is an instrument of influence on a child. Everybody knows that a surgeon's scalpel must be razor-sharp and sterile and that his hands must not shake. What is the tool of a psychotherapist? He himself is his tool.

In society, all of us are used to trying to hide our inner problems. At first I thought this was a good thing. I would say, 'If you tell yourself long enough that you are open and sociable, then that's how you will become.' Now, however, I'm not so sure. In fact, I doubt it. Pretending to oneself means that it is not oneself that is presented to the world, but some kind of a ghost or double. Any feedback that is directed at this ghost doesn't touch the real person. We don't look inside of ourselves, at our soul, but at an abstraction that's divorced from our 'bad side'. I have been in many situations like that. I might be talking to someone from the heart when suddenly he says about himself, 'I'm not a leader. I hate taking responsibility. I'm weak, but I watch others to try to learn from them', and so on. Then I realise that he is like a painting. He is not revealing himself but is drawing a picture for me of a different character. Our conversation has become like some kind of abstract, aesthetic exercise; just lies and artifice.

We can draw this phantom over and over as much as we like, giving it positive qualities and leaving out the negative. The trouble is that it doesn't derive from true consciousness but from a kind of secure compartment. For a child, the role-playing process can be quite useful, as far as it allows her to understand within a conversation what is 'good' and what is 'bad'. But for an adult with the habit of clinging to the safe and comfortable in his inner world, such psychological games can be self-deceptive and harmful.

We can only accept into our community, therefore, people who are genuinely ready to open themselves up to those around them and who can share their genuine inner world and not some abstract ideal. It can be difficult and painful. It requires will, determination and discipline. When do you not need discipline? In battle? In the workshop? You need it everywhere.

Thus, every adult in Kitezh is part of the developing environment and they are expected to put forth their best efforts to meet the following guidelines:

Discuss all problems of relationships with children and other adults openly. Place the unity of the community and the interests of the children before self.

Avoid remarks and actions that could prompt the children to form a negative view of the world.

Involve people's feelings in their work and continually exchange ideas and information among the group.

Working in a therapeutic community means accepting the importance of inner work and accepting the guidance and criticism of colleagues as given in the daily Teachers' Council and by the elected director. A colleague who has not made progress in resolving his inner problems and complexes cannot be a good teacher or psychologist. Being open to lifelong personal development and possessing a good-hearted nature, inner peace, clarity of mind, and purity of purpose—all are necessary qualities that earn one the right to work with the inner world of children.

Adults in Kitezh are able to spend more time with children, and more intensively, than in other educational institutions. Thus, every child is subject to a more intensive educational influence in countless informal situations every day. The Teachers' Council tries to foresee these informal situations and prepare everyone with a plan of action for every child. Each day we keep an eye out for emotional and psychological changes in our children that give rise to particular concerns or alert us to acute difficulties. This individual approach means constant discussion on the part of the adults, a constant exchange of information between teachers, parents and other staff members. We can then establish a succession of obstacles and challenges for each child that responds to his or her particular needs and problems as they change.

Every step forward is a step into the unknown. Perhaps it is a dangerous unknown. Adults may be hesitant to release their old convictions, stereotypes, fallacies and hopes. Moving to Kitezh means giving up one's former, easier life, but it corresponds to laws on which the natural world is based. It is the path to personal development. We need courage to look in the mirror. We need will power to overcome our sluggishness, our indifference and our reluctance to exert ourselves. This movement forward would not be possible without support from those around us.

What the community needs is creative people. We need creative bakers; creative farmers; creative foster parents. Our collective well-being—and perhaps more importantly, the overall atmosphere in our community—depends on everyone being involved. Everyone participates in building houses, making decisions, and helping shape our common future. Each of us must be able to perceive problems, find creative solutions, and harmonise our vision with that of everyone else so that life's inevitable twists and turns do not sink our common ship.

7

Therapeutic Community

Kitezh has grown organically. At the outset, it was a community first and a professional facility for orphaned children second. We now see the opportunity to move on from this position and have for the last four years actively sought to establish a sound professional base for our work, as was always intended.

One must keep in mind several factors about Russia's orphan situation. First, for many years, there were no alternatives to state institutions. Second, because of our history and culture, our orphan problem is perhaps the greatest of any nation in the world. Third, the term 'orphan' in Russia refers to children who have been removed from their parents for their own safety as well as children whose parents have died.

Kitezh is a conscious move away from a system that has been creaking and crumbling for decades, and that takes little or no account of the spiritual or individual needs of the child. Kitezh is small. We believe strongly that education is an essential therapeutic tool, and that the very fabric and rhythm of our daily life is therapy. In other words, we are the antithesis of the state institutions.

In state-run orphanages, therapy is dispensed by white-coated psychologists as a medical prescription. That is the last thing we do. Our kids communicate ceaselessly with adults and among themselves; they play free of external dangers such as traffic and unwelcome or predatory advances. They have realistic expectations placed upon them; and they have adults who are prepared to wait, for as long as it takes, until they are ready to take full advantage of the education they are offered.

Our children are supported in their normal and not so normal developmental steps and cared for in our unique foster families. Although each of our foster families has its own distinctive structure, in many of them the foster parents' natural children live and work alongside the orphans, as if they were their biological siblings. Kitezh has created a dynamic and psychotherapeutic group environment, and while we face many challenges, we are moving steadily towards what may be Russia's first residential therapeutic community for children who have suffered difficult conditions early in their lives.

You may have heard that in Siberia and elsewhere in Russia a number of communities have been established that bear the hallmarks of sects or cults. Recently there has been a good amount of unhelpful evangelising by foreigners in our country that is aimed at our most vulnerable populations. Although Kitezh does have a spiritual basis, it is in no way a cult, a sect, or an evangelising agent.

In his report following his visit to Kitezh as a consultant in April 2003, David Dean noted that the Charterhouse Group defines a therapeutic community as 'a group of people who live or meet together regularly and participate together in a range of useful tasks—therapeutic, domestic, organisational, educational. Another criterion is a shared commitment to the goal of learning from the experience of living and/or working together in a living, learning situation. How does Kitezh measure up to this? Very well indeed. In fact, I would maintain that Kitezh life…meets this criteria as well as, if not better than, many of the British communities.'

Two major differences between Kitezh and British therapeutic communities are that not all of Kitezh's staff are paid, and not all of its members possess skills that extend much beyond the basic competency level. Despite this deficit, an unusual and encouraging phenomenon is taking shape. The first wave of young adults who spent a number of their formative years in Kitezh are now playing an active role in the life and therapeutic work of the community. They take part in an intensive, well-supervised, and consistently applied programme of mentoring and group discussion. Members of what we call the Small Council, consisting of six fifteen to eighteen-year-olds, are gradually inducted into practising therapeutic skills with younger children with greater success than some of the adults.

We are still in our relative infancy and I don't want to make grandiose claims, but I have observed extraordinary growth in the leadership abilities of our children. Every second day, we conduct what we call the Children's Meeting for an hour after dinner. All who are present—children as well as adults—are invited to speak about their experiences, successes, disappointments and emotions since the last meeting. Participants are patient, positive, engaged in the process, and mindful of the right of each speaker to be heard and responded to.

This and the myriad of other routinely positive interactions in Kitezh—the culture of play for the younger children; the generally appropriate interactions among the adolescents—make it a place where time is very well spent. There is no delinquency, no violence, and no intentional disturbances. We must conclude, therefore, that the blend of natural and foster children, together with the milieu created by that mix, cannot really be compared with the client group of any British therapeutic community of which I am aware.

Kitezh

PHYSICAL FEATURES

If you were to find yourself in Kitezh right now, you would see log cabins with turrets, carved pine porches, ornamental carved window decorations, and delicate little wooden bridges. It is as if a picture by the Russian artist Vasnetsov had come to life. Charming as this fairytale setting may be, however, it has a serious purpose, for we believe it plays an important role in enabling our children to be receptive to fairy tales. Why is an interest in fairy tales relevant? Because it is only in the world of fable that metamorphoses, miracles and transformations are possible. The settlement we have built functions as an instrument that allows us to work with the subconscious. Our very name, as I have mentioned before, has been taken from folklore. Kitezh was a mythical invisible town transformed by the will of God into a vessel of spiritual energy.

The traditional Russian architecture of Kitezh makes the child conscious of the good and equitable world of fairy tales. It allows him to feel a sense of affinity with his native land and people and it reconnects him with his roots, thus helping to prevent him from feeling lonely and lost. The style of the architecture, the pictures on the walls of the houses, our tradition of occasionally dressing in embroidered Russian shirts, the singing of folk songs on festive occasions—all have a part to play in relieving emotional problems. We turn to the most deeply embedded images from folk culture, fairy tales and myth to build a picture of the world. We are no more inclined to talk about Jung's theory of the collective subconscious than a fish is inclined to analyse the water in which it swims. Nevertheless, there are grounds to believe that this collective subconscious is a powerful force that is often worth harnessing for the benefit of the developing environment.

Mythology is essential. In Kitezh the child undergoes a complex process that amounts to virtually a complete change in his worldview. During this process he is very vulnerable. He is required to reconsider and revise many of his assumptions about life. He may feel ashamed about his former way of life and may try to erase particularly painful memories relating to theft, violence, or sexual experiences. It is possible that having rejected his old assumptions about life, the child is left with nothing at all with which to construct a new value system. In such a case, secular images from early childhood that encourage him to believe that there is goodness, equity and love in the world can be a point of reference. What is it that lies at the very heart of most of our beloved fairy tales? It is the idea that magical transformations are possible and the most important thing that happens at Kitezh is the magical transformation of our children.

To create a permanent natural background that testifies to the existence of beauty and order in the world, we draw upon the charm of the lime tree-lined avenues of the ancient park, the calm of the shady ponds, the carefully laid-out and well-kept paved paths, and the flower beds around the houses. The children participate actively in the creation of this beautiful environment and in doing so they discover a simple truth: that it is within their power to change their world and that they themselves can fill their lives with beauty and order. Thus foundations are laid for feelings of patriotism and love towards one's native land. At the same time, the children learn to derive energy from their everyday physical surroundings.

The ideal would be that every object in a child's home triggered an emotional response, an appreciation of its aesthetic qualities. The traditional rural way of life went some way towards meeting this ideal. People carved utensils; made and decorated boxes, sleighs and crockery; and made colourful and decorative needlework. In this way, commonplace items were transformed into artistic objects that were a delight to look at. The seasonal cycle of work and festivals was connected to the higher laws of the universe or nature, which in turn transformed everyday life into a purposeful ritual.

Even Western scholars are beginning to recognise the simple truth, acknowledged by the ancient Hindus, that a person's psychological being requires nourishment in exactly the same way as does his physical self. Parents who are preoccupied with material well-being view the task of caring for their child in material terms, such as paying for their education and foreign trips. They insist that their children study hard. In terms of formal logic, there is nothing wrong with this but our world is much more complex than this allows for and such a one-dimensional approach fails to respond to all of a child's needs.

Man as a biological species has been evolving for millions of years. It is only now, as industry and information technology are rapidly developing, that we are being cosseted and cocooned. Perhaps our incessant use of the computer and the television will trigger the evolution of a new species, one that draws energy directly from an electronic display, but that will not happen any time soon. Our children, as did the children who went before them, require nourishment from the living world. No 'Mountain Air Ionisers' or photographs from *The National Geographic* can replace having green grass under foot and the opportunity to see the clouds, tall trees and distant mountains. We are born into a living world and unless our children engage with this world they will not develop as they should.

The natural surrounding of Kitezh and its intricately designed log cabins are constant sources of joy and wonder. Yet many children actually need to be taught how to appreciate it. On the basis of what we have observed, it appears that foster children can live in Kitezh for a number of years and still not learn how to take pleasure from the beauty that is all around them.

Every normal person can expect at least once in their life to experience the curative force of nature—the way it hones the senses and suffuses one's being with energy. Sometimes the ability to contemplate beauty and to feel at one with the mighty forces of the sky and the earth becomes a means of survival, a way to maintain a healthy state of mind.

We are not referring here to the sentimental attachment of the town-dweller to the great outdoors, but to the fact that instead of turning to medication or drugs, every person can use the powerful resource that is nature. Our fields, park and forests amount to more than just our habitat and the basis of our material survival. They are also a source of our inner strength. They remind us of life's great and endlessly changing ebb and flow and provide welcome signs of the everlasting nature of the world of which all of Kitezh's residents sense they are a part.

'I don't know what my inner world is like. My mama and papa don't talk to me about it, but I am very afraid when they shout,' Lyosha, aged thirteen.

In Kitezh, the child is offered a holistic model of the world that is based on goodness and fairness, but a pack of wolves or a computer can also provide an educational environment. The personality will not develop successfully unless a person feels a connection to another person, and through this a connection to mankind as a whole.

8

The Family

FOSTERED CHILDREN

The children who are placed at Kitezh have endured extremely unpleasant and painful experiences from which even adults might find it impossible to recover. These children do not believe in the rationality and primordial goodness of the world. Drunken parents may have deprived them of food and have rewarded them with beatings. They may have been caught by the police in a basement and sent off to child detention centres. They may have been forced by their teachers to sit through unnecessary lessons. In order to survive, they have had to learn to fight, not to trust anyone, to hide, and to steal food and money. By and large, the adult world is a hostile and alien place for these children.

A particular feature of human cognition is that in a given environment the mind will first register information that has already been processed and is familiar. New information is not registered in the same way and consequently can remain unconscious for a fairly long time. Consistently during the last ten years, children arriving at Kitezh have not initially noticed the deep contrasts between their new and old environments. In their first analysis of the community they simply establish that the adults do not use bad language or hit the children. This is as far as their assessment goes. Assured of his personal safety, the child resumes his usual behaviour, with absolutely no intention of learning new rules and ideas.

The children living side by side with us have simply refused to recognise the new reality, responding only to the kind of confrontational words and situations that convinced them of the fundamental immutability of the nature of the world as they perceived it in the first place. It often seems that formerly homeless children are so completely overwhelmed by their unhappy memories that they are continuously testing their new world for durability, wanting and trying to convince themselves that it is essentially ephemeral.

Every new child has started out by fighting for his place in the pecking order by trying to suppress the weaker members. Those who used to smoke have continued to smoke, and those who used to steal have continued to steal. In addition, what surprisingly elaborate use they have made of bad language when they have thought that the adults could not hear! Two worlds have been evident in Kitezh: the civilised world of the adults and the cruel world of the children. These two worlds existed as if in isolation from each other, not meshing together. Although the first generation of our foster children lived among us, they did not live with us, as part of the community. The community of adults functioned as a separate entity while the children moved back and forth between their foster parents and teachers, interacting with both groups of adults but not sensing the integrity of the social order.

We thought the children would automatically accept the view of the world and the values of the adults. We somehow forgot that this is far from always the case. It was only gradually that we realised that to live together does not mean to share ideals. The greatest dream of the first children was to grow up and leave Kitezh, move to Moscow and earn a lot of money so that they could be independent and free. The advice given by their adult mentors did not help and any disciplinary action only convinced the children that they were right in believing that the fundamental nature of the world was the same as in their former environments. Interactions and relationships were still grounded in violence and conflict.

When we became aware of this pattern, we began to look for approaches to modify the children's deeply ingrained perceptions. It had become clear that attempts at persuasion as well as coercion were altogether useless. It was apparent that rather than simply erasing the child's existing picture of the world, it would be necessary to provide him with a new, brighter, and enduring view of the world. It is with this, and not the re-education of each individual child, that the Kitezh therapeutic community is concerned.

Children only notice what they are accustomed to and therefore do not see their new foster parents objectively. If they do form a perspective, it is usually not the one that we would wish.

I have yet to come across an ideal foster family. Some have lacked competency, while others have been absorbed with their own domestic or psychological problems. Some have lavished such attention on the children that they have been unable to follow the path that would be right for them. For many adults who do hard physical work, it is difficult to switch from thinking about their own problems to considering those of the children. This means that Kitezh families are also far from ideal. Moreover, each family has its own particular strengths and weaknesses. This is why we give the children the right to choose and change their foster families. While we believe that this is the epitome of democracy, certain adults have been somewhat offended by the idea that it is the parents who should try to meet the needs of the children and not the other way around. Parents seldom think about the impression that their appearance has on a child. We asked our children to tell us about their first impressions of their foster parents.

I was scared living with foster mother X. She didn't brush her hair and she looked strange. Sometimes she was simply terrifying. And then there was Larissa who was big and warm. Sometimes I wished that she was my mama.

I don't like it when my papa doesn't shave and he smells worse than my mama.

These kinds of observations suggest that foster fathers should shave and both parents should brush their hair and make sure they smell nice. They should be soft and smooth, both literally and in a figurative sense, meaning that they should refrain from loud laughter and crude adult jokes.

One of the main things that a new foster parent will discover is that the child will make no attempt whatsoever to be grateful for everything the foster parent has done for them. To the care provider, it seems that if they feed, sing to, and speak kindly to their foster child, he will inevitably recognise their love, perceive the vast goodness of their nature, and accept their view of the world. Foster parents, however, should put themselves in the child's place. The child will remember that he was refused a football, made to sit down and study, and so on. He sees signs that the foster parent cares about him, but his personal life experience cries out, 'Don't believe it! Don't trust them!' It is truly sad, but it is a child's core life experience that forms the starting point from which he judges the world. It may take a child years to learn to trust the people who love him.

If you were to find yourself on a battlefield or in a concentration camp, you would begin to understand what it is like for a young person, who is used to living within the protection of his family, to be placed within the confines of a children's home. The need to defend himself from aggression and hide his feelings is exceptionally stressful. It is openness that makes a young person vulnerable to his contemporaries, so the child puts up defences and learns how to protect himself, which isolates him from a whole stream of information about the external world. He is deprived of the opportunity to form relationships openly with other children and is forced to go along with the pack. He is afraid of hearing what other people think about him, does not cultivate emotional relationships with others as a child normally would, and is afraid of forming trusting relationships.

We were moved in the first years of our work at Kitezh by the sight of children following on the heels of their foster parents as they hurried off to work. It took us a while to realise that the children were following their parents out of fear of losing them and in an effort to ensure their safety. The parents should take time to accustom their child to the idea that they will always come back and that he will not lose them. Unless a child goes through this exercise in trust he will never be able to overcome his feelings of anxiety, and this in turn will impinge upon his development.

PHILLIP'S STORY (PART TWO)

Phillip has lived with a foster family for five years now. He would often say he loved Kitezh and his new parents. At the time in question, he was in Class Six and he was in the habit of helping his parents out around the house. He was, he said, content with his life. But then a new young lad, Slava, arrived at Kitezh. Slava taught Phillip how to play table tennis, and what is more, Slava had time to play every evening. Phillip saw this as a reason to dodge his evening studies and devote himself to the game. A month later, when Slava left the community, little Phillip made it known that he wanted to go with him. He dropped everyone! 'He lost interest in both his friends and his family,' commented one of his classmates.

What happened? The child found a vein of pure joy that, in his immature cognitive development, was associated with a single person, and he lost interest in everyone else. For five years he has lived his life according to the principle of 'here and now', responding only when something required his immediate attention, not thinking about the consequences of his actions or accumulating experience, instead repeating the same mistakes over and over again. He is good at carrying out orders like 'bring some firewood' or 'help Mama do the dishes', but he is incapable of sustained effort and of working independently without supervision. Left on his own, he is unable to make himself study, even though he fully understands that there would be repercussions if he fails to do his homework. This type of behaviour is typical of orphaned children who have experienced emotional trauma at a young age.

In order to understand the laws of our good, free world, a child must erase his old views of the world, a view that has been painfully engraved into every cell of his body. He must forget about restrictions. He must savor the taste of unrestricted freedom, albeit only at certain times and in certain places. For example, he can be given an hour to do whatever he wants in his room (apart from setting it on fire), or when he is out on a hike he can be told he may sleep out under the stars, go wherever he wants, and try anything he takes a fancy to. This will reduce the extent to which he is tempted by something simply because it is forbidden. Even sweets will gradually lose their appeal if they are freely available and in such circumstances the mind can free itself for other desires. Left to his own devices, he will feel secure and start to show interest in his surroundings. True, he will not yet reject his long-held view of the world, but he will at least develop a realistic appreciation of restrictions and prohibitions.

It should be remembered that the actions and reactions of children speak louder than their actual words. In recognition of this fact, a system of play therapy has been devised, which allows the psychotherapist to draw conclusions about the psychological well-being of a child simply by observing how he or she plays with various toys.

PLAY THERAPY

The room is full of toys. The child may pick up any toy and play as he wants. An adult observes the child at play and does whatever the child tells him to. Sometimes the adult asks the child questions. The aim of this whole exercise is to give the child the chance to play out that which is lurking in the depths of his mind and that is preventing him from seeing that which is real.

Nina laid some dolls out on the floor in one long row. 'Who are they?' the psychologist asked. 'They are my teachers from the children's home,' replied Nina, and she picked up a plastic sabre and started methodically to slash the doll's legs. Smiling sweetly, she said, 'And this is so that they don't come after me.'

Then there was Zhenya. He set up all the toy soldiers in a row and started kicking them. He repeated it day after day. Then, during the last session, he started playing 'families' with the dolls' house. I would like to say that he has never shown aggression since then, never fought or sworn. There have been relapses but he has definitely become calmer and started to work better and to listen to other people's opinions, even when these weren't accompanied by a clenched fist.

Lena underwent a course of play therapy with Marina, who

was training as a play therapist with Chris, a British professional. The first thing that was striking was the extreme degree of self-control demonstrated by the six-year-old girl. The emotions, which she undoubtedly felt, were not reflected in her face, not even when, for the first time in her life, she entered a room full of toys. Life had taught her to avoid falling into traps set by adults. As any secret agent would tell you, revealing one's emotions makes a person vulnerable. Adults had ensured that Lena was well aware of this. When she realises that adults are waiting for her to show her emotions, she will demonstrate them readily, acting out whole scenarios with her facial expressions but in actual fact she does not understand what emotion she should be showing, and when she should be showing it. As a result, she also doesn't understand the emotions of the people with whom she has contact.

A child brought up in a normal family generally will not feel threatened, and will, therefore, be open to the world and able to interact with it directly. Let me tell you what can be surmised about Lena's past. On the basis of the facts available to us, it seems that her mother considered her very existence to be an inconvenience. When the little girl demanded attention she was punished so she learned to control her emotions, but this was a terribly exhausting process. Even now she still tries to work out what emotion she should show and exactly how she should show it; in the end she is too drained to actually feel the emotion. Pretending to be her mother, Lena would put a doll in the bath and then forget it, leaving it in the cold water, or she would lock a doll up in the bathroom of the doll's house. When she participated in this type of role play about her family, disturbing memories surfaced in the little girl. As a result, sometimes she would ask the therapists whether they would like to play, and sometimes she would herself end the role play and pick up different toys instead.

I am not in possession of sufficient information to be able to unravel the endless sequence of images and associations that come to light during play therapy, and indeed it is beyond the scope of this book. I would simply point out that a lot of translated specialist literature on this subject is now available. What I would like you to appreciate, however, is that the child will develop at an early age awareness and knowledge of the world using his senses, and figuratively speaking, the world will take on the hue of his emotions. If these emotions are suppressed, then the child's world will become devoid of colour and, in some cases, his perceptions of the world will actually become distorted. A child who can play out a situation in a room in the form of a game and, at a later stage, in his mind, will be able to rid himself of many of his fears and start to live a normal and emotionally rich life.

I could claim with pride that I discovered play therapy right at the beginning of the 1970s! It's a pity that I didn't patent it. When I came home from school I would take out my tin soldiers and replay those moments from the day that I would have liked to have changed, leading my army to victory, crushing my enemies and saving the classmates that I liked. Of course my parents laughed, not comprehending what I was doing. In this way, play is a natural psychotherapy. For many, this process later becomes transformed into writing, art, or another creative activity.

I could have fallen into idle daydreaming if it were not for the fact that I was blessed with strong, purposeful parents who did not believe in religion or the Communist Party, or indeed anything except honest labour and the development of one's intellectual abilities. Because they provided me with a consistent example and intentionally put me under pressure ('Study! Exercise! Read!'), I was occasionally able to enjoy the sweet taste of victory over my own weakness.

My parents did not make unkind comparisons between

myself and the ever-so-popular Russian folktale character, Ivan the Fool, nor did they quote the proverbs that became a damning legacy, such as 'you should stick to what you are good at' or 'you can't build a bridge over the ocean'. They always insisted that I stretch myself to the limit of my modest capabilities, were never entirely satisfied with my achievements, and forced me to strive upwards and onwards. I tried to resist the pressure, and in the course of doing so unwittingly strengthened my character. As they used to tell us in history class at school, 'It is in battle that you come into your own.'

It wasn't until secondary school that I started to get Bs instead of Cs, but I had little interest in my grades. I knew that the principal challenge ahead of me would be studying at Lomonosov Moscow State University. I rose to this challenge too, and it was then that I finally believed in my ability to overcome obstacles. Could that have been why I devoted myself to building Kitezh?

The will to achieve is cultivated so that it gradually becomes a conditioned reflex. What is most important is that life be full of challenges, victories (even if only occasional), and encouragement. It is not through punishment but encouragement that we acquire the habit of turning resolute mental effort into something that comes as naturally as breathing.

9

The Right to Life's Experience

My son Svyatoslav was three-and-a-half. He loved messing around with his twelve-year-old brother, Vasya. Besides deriving happiness from their games, he was assured of their equal status: 'Give me the teddy! Chase me! Catch me! Oi, don't touch me!' They would play, pushing each other and giggling hysterically. One evening, Vasya got tired and told Svyatoslav it was time for bed, but Svetik (short for Svyatoslav) brushed aside the idea. Vasya tried to be more persistent. Svetik punched him and stood in his way, which of course provoked retaliation. Vasya shoved him back. That really started it! Shrieking, indignation... 'Ow, you hurt me! I hate you!'

Our attempts to reason with him—'but you were laughing when he hit you, and you hit him first'—had no effect. Svetik would have none of it. He sulked all evening, and grumbled that Vasya had hurt him. Even Vasya, somehow feeling that he had done something wrong, started to apologise. Irina tried long and hard to explain to Svetik that a playful shove is no reason to get angry with someone. In his mind, however, Svetik had very clearly differentiated between the shoving during the game and that last shove with which Vasya had tried to put him in his place. It hadn't hurt him physically but emotionally it was an affront. Svetik wasn't able to tell us this. He continued to be affected by this injustice for much longer than a physical wound would last. A week later he still reminded us of how hurt he was.

A month went by and it seemed that he had forgotten it. Then, suddenly, early one morning, Svetik decided he was going to be 'a good boy' and started to list his resolutions: 'I'll do what I'm told, I'll eat everything, and I won't cry'. Then, amid all these positive changes, we suddenly hear, '…and I won't be angry with Vasya any more for hitting me.'

'This already sounds like a phobia,' my wife said, alarmed.

'Maybe it means that once it's marked in his consciousness, he can't erase it,' I replied. 'That's how information is built up about the injustice and right and wrong. What else has he got stored up there that we don't know about? What have we missed that will rise to the surface in ten years?'

'What if we got into the archive where he filed away this silly argument and erase it?'

'You can't erase it. That archive is full of essential memories. That must be the reason why the Creator protected every individual system. Otherwise there would be all these programmers who could get into our individual database.'

'So how can we get him to forget about this thing with Vasya?'

'He'll grow up and see what had happened. He already started this morning to revise his own programme. "I'm going to be good!" That means he wants to evaluate his behaviour. He's got this innate gift for going over what he's done.'

But does he have sufficient strength of character and courage to look inside himself and see the error in his programme?

Every moment we spend with our child is an important lesson. In many cases, it is either an obvious or a hidden challenge to our inventiveness, our patience and our empathy. When we set up this invisible contact with our child, we see that the interaction becomes closer and closer. Our intuition will tell us the best responses.

I think we need to remember two mutually exclusive truths.

First, a child's freedom and independence from his parents allows him to rely on his own strengths and gain essential life experience so that he makes independent choices that reflect his inner nature. Second, the intensity and depth of a child's relationship with his parents directly influences the speed and complexity of his development, so that the more you talk to and spend time with him, the more actively he will develop.

'What I like most about my dad is that he's kind. That's all. He doesn't have any bad features,' Andrei, age twelve.

As described in Chapter Eight, one of the major discoveries that await you in your relationship with a foster child is that his life experience is his starting point for his judgment of the world. It might take years for your child to learn to trust those who love him.

Here I would like to distinguish between three groups of foster children who will have been affected differently by their early circumstances:

1. The 'safe' option

Before taking your chosen child into your family, find out as much as you can about the first years of his life. If he has received loving attention from his parents, especially his mother in his earliest years, he will have formed a positive image of family life, at least subconsciously, and he will have an experience of forming an attachment to his mother. What remains for you to do is to reconcile this image of the world with the truth that surrounds him and so convince him that he has already found what he was striving for subconsciously.

If he was lucky enough to get this initial image of love, at least in his early experience, then he will recognise love and accept it in his new family. By the way, the same applies to your own biological children. There is a new tradition of mothers keeping a distance from their small children and teaching them to be socially convenient. If parents don't teach their little children how to feel love and how to give and receive love freely, then their own children will inherit the problem and recreate it within their own families. I say this because I have studied about fifty personal cases of adults who were unable to create a family based on love because they didn't receive this initial image from their own parents.

If your child comes to your family straight after losing his parents, he won't yet have become unused to domestic life. This will make it easier for him to understand what you want from him in daily life, but all the same, you will have to determine what he is able to do and what he is used to. Don't try to reform his habits too soon. Try to build understanding and mutual trust upon the foundation of his accepted and familiar patterns of behaviour. This is much more important than making him follow rules of conduct that might seem normal to you. Equally, don't relax too much. After a couple of weeks or months the honeymoon period will be over, and your child will start to put your reliability to the test.

2. Children from orphanages

In the previous chapter, we likened the experience of a very young personality who is used to the protection his family provides and who suddenly ends up in an orphanage to the kind of shock you would experience on a battlefield or in a concentration camp. The child is placed under extreme psychological stress; suddenly he needs to defend himself from external aggression and to hide his feelings. He learns immediately that sincerity in his emotions makes him vulnerable to teasing and humiliation. The child clams up, learns to protect himself, and at the same time shuts out all incoming information from the outside world. He is deprived of the ability to form friendships easily with other children and is forced to live, as it were, in a herd of children with whom he is in constant competition for attention. He becomes fearful of feedback, sealed from emotional contact, and afraid of building trust.

Children who have lived in an orphanage become aware very early in life of the limits to their abilities, which rob them of a critical human characteristic: the ambition to develop their abilities or the urge to self-development. This is why foster parents are obliged above all else to fill a therapeutic role. They must become for their child a symbol of a new reality that affords him the freedom from anxiety, fear and guilt.

3. Children from the wilderness

Children in this category have experienced life without guardianship, perhaps on the streets or in an orphanage, where they have had such pitifully inadequate care that they will literally have had to fight for their survival. Such a child tends to be focused and active, with strong adult qualities even by the age of eleven or twelve—you grow up fast when you must look after yourself. He also will have formed his personal, and probably malevolent and disparaging view of the adult world. He will be able to assimilate new information that configures with his image of the world easily, and quickly adapt to changing circumstances. He will quickly assess who is dangerous, and where the opportunities are. But no matter what he sees in his new family surroundings, his perception will be tainted by his ingrained negative worldview. It is extremely difficult to earn his trust or love, as he simply will not believe your good intentions and he will see through your attempts to soften his character and instill in him a new, more socially acceptable, view of the world. If he suddenly begins to behave obediently and impress you with his gentle language, it may be a purposeful effort at manipulation in order to gain a particular end.

The last thing you should do is to try and change him with admonitions or by showering him with presents. Persuading a child through incentives is rarely a good idea, especially if he is already weak-willed: he may become utterly dependent upon you and unable to derive satisfaction from his own accomplishments. The inability to feel satisfaction is common in abandoned children.

This danger has arisen in Kitezh. We have seen our children obediently follow the daily routine, take part in clubs and extracurricular activities and organise plays and shows. Among them were a group of boys who, although they took part in everything as long as they felt the force of obligation, the only real pleasure they got was from smoking together.

In order to accept the laws of your good, free world, the fostered child has to clean the slate of his previous image of the world, which was etched with pain into every cell of his body. He needs to forget about the limitations he is used to feeling trapped by, and learn to feel unlimited freedom. Let him sleep if he wants to, play, eat; above all let him feel free to do what he wants to do. As the desire for the formerly forbidden becomes boring the mind is freed for greater ambitions.

Initially if such a child is allowed to adjust in his own time, he will gradually feel safe and begin to demonstrate an interest in his surroundings. He will not completely reject the old world that he knows, but at least he will accept the relativity of its limitations. In addition be prepared to make his life less convenient, and fill it with challenges, which will guarantee his development.

THE HONEYMOON IS OVER

Your child has been living with you for a few weeks or months. He has become used to the daily routine, has learned where everything is in your house, what tasty things he will find in the fridge, how to persuade you to let him watch television, and so on. You can expect the end of the honeymoon any time now. He has, after all, only just got to know you and figured out what he likes about life at your place. Still, he needs much more: he needs to create a safe attachment. He must convince himself that he can depend on you so that he can rid himself of the fear that you will also disappear from his life.

However good and understanding foster parents may be, there will still always be a degree of anxiety in a child who has once been psychologically damaged over whether his present surroundings will also disappoint his expectations—whether his parents will betray him or abandon him again.

At the start it seemed to us that any child who had lived a few months in Kitezh would be convinced of the reliability of her new parents and friends and that this trust and confidence would help her reconstruct her perception of the world. For instance, Anna who I will say more about later, would not change her initial criteria for evaluation and continued from one year to the next to measure events by her own yardstick, refused to refute her former circumstances and constantly found confirmation of her negative perception of the world— 'You won't buy me that doll, because you don't love me.' A close relationship between adult and child is essential for the child to be able to develop an image of a good and non-threatening world.

Lisa joined a family at the age of six. Although they had no previous experience in bringing up children, her foster parents approached their new responsibility with great seriousness and sense of purpose. They bathed and clothed their new daughter, read her stories, and taught her to help around the house, but they did not connect with her in any profound way. Abiding by her foster mother's household routine seemed to help Lisa settle in somewhat, but it did nothing to help her overcome her root problems.

Among these problems were an alcoholic mother who tried to get rid of her daughter at any price and a traumatic separation from her elder sister. Lisa regarded her foster family as a temporary shelter and spent the ensuing six years looking for substitutes for her mother and especially her sister. In her new family she found a potential elder sister, but this girl was preoccupied with her own problems and left for Moscow to continue her education. Complicating the situation was the contentious situation between Lisa's foster parents and other families in the community stemming from their refusal to cooperate with the Educational Council which, if not resolved, could lead to them having to leave the community.

When Lisa was thirteen, a crisis erupted. During a community celebration, she broke down and became hysterical. Attempts by adults to comfort her and understand what was wrong got nowhere. Lisa closed up like an oyster. Finally, seventeen-year-old Sasha managed to gain her trust and listened to her tearful explanation: 'I want to live in your family.' It's not that Lisa wanted new parents—any parent would be a source of anxiety and uncertainty. What she wanted was an older sister, and she did not want to be forced to leave Kitezh with her foster parents.

After a month of discussion within the Educational Council, Lisa decided to move to another family. Her new foster mother was the youngest mother in the community at that time, and to some extent could be seen as an older sister. Upon arriving in her new family the first thing Lisa said was, 'I'll do all the household chores but please don't write out a rota and don't make me follow a daily routine.' She now found herself in a family that was more dynamic and open to spontaneity and the willingness to respond and develop. After three months, Lisa started bursting into tears frequently and displaying nervous reactions. She became jealous and hurt and refused to accept her parents' help with homework. The problems locked away in her subconscious had begun to emerge.

Then, at Christmas, Lisa was taken to a nearby monastery to be baptised. She chose the strongest, most intelligent and reliable girl from Year Ten to be her godmother, who gladly accepted because she already had a lot of experience of helping her younger sister. In this way Lisa achieved the attachment she craved, between sisters and not parent and child.

In a city, complex relationships such as these would make life very difficult. In Kitezh, however, where in the children's subconscious we are one big family, this form of attachment gave Lisa the opportunity to restore her self-respect and faith in the world. She soon exhibited a more open relationship with her new foster parents, newfound confidence at school, and a willingness to actively participate in amateur dramatic performances. Three months after her christening, she played the leading role in a school play, and two weeks after that, for the first time, she asked her mother for help with her history homework, a subject she had always found particularly difficult. On the following day she received her first top grade to the thunderous applause of her classmates. She went straight home and scrubbed the floors, did the laundry, and repaired a broken cupboard door. She still needs assurances of her significance and to feel a safe attachment to all the members of her new family.

Lisa's new foster parents endured a difficult six months before she felt truly settled with them. A child often hides unmet needs and it is difficult to know exactly what it is that is blocking her natural development. We recommend that parents wait for the inevitable crisis to emerge and then carefully analyse the problem behind it.

Always be ready to be tested. A child has to test and make

certain of the reality of the surroundings they find themselves in. When foster parents take a child into their family and the testing starts, they must help the child overcome his fear and feelings of rejection. A child must get used to the fact that he has the right to choose and that his actions will not result in criticism and punishment. If a child learns to confide in you about all of his fears without worrying whether you will laugh at or judge him, then he will be able to let go of those fears.

ANNA'S STORY

Anna grew up without a father. Her mother was a lady of the night and was often not in a fit state to look after even herself, let alone her daughter. Consequently Anna learned the necessity of controlling her own mother. In Kitezh she chose to leave two families because she refused to accept either of the women who had tried to assume the role of her foster mother and had rejected their overtures to build a relationship based on trust and affection. Her previous experience taught her that women who pose as mothers are not to be trusted. After three years, she chose another foster mother herself, but refused to talk to her about her problems and kept strictly to herself. She resisted any psychological probing or heart-to-heart discussions and preferred to put direct pressure on her mother to get sweets and new things out of her.

She distrusted her new mother to such an extent that she proudly refused any help with her homework, which the other children considered invaluable. On top of this, every day she would look for an excuse to make a scene—refusing to get up, to eat, to comb her hair, and so forth. In the first place, quarrelling with her mother helped her attain a degree of control over events in the home. Second, it was a perverse means of protecting herself from potential aggression by her mother. She knew that while she was having a tantrum, her mother wouldn't remember to make her do her homework, and that afterwards there was always time to say sorry, have a cry and kiss and make up.

When looking after a loved one, it is an important thing not to try too hard, otherwise your fussing will become a hindrance to her development. Your effort to forge a secure relationship must not rob the child of her initiative and her ability or willingness to take risks. Parent-child relationships that are too comfortable do not provide enough stimuli for those who do not wish to grow up. It is imperative that a child does not get the idea that he is a little prince and you are his servant or he will find endless ways to manipulate you. It is a curious paradox that your little boy may do badly at school and can't string two words together, yet is swift to figure out how to get his favourite sausages at tea time or get out of doing his reading or the washing up. If you let him know that you are not to be messed with, the temptation to become a spoiled little prince and a cynical manipulator may be avoided. If you are strong-minded, you can withstand any test. You will need unbounded patience because even if you win a quarrel with your child today, there is no guarantee of victory tomorrow.

Let us return to Anna. After a year of living with her new foster mother, she started to talk about moving on again. The older boys and girls, in the best tradition of our community, talked to her about her behaviour. In this there is an element of positive peer pressure, which we call peer support. Anna was accustomed to ignoring her mother's admonitions, but remarks like 'you'll always be a little girl if you don't act more grown-up' and 'none of the boys will want to talk to you if you're always so awkward and childish', coming from other children, had a strong influence on the ten-year-old, and she decided to change.

Suddenly, life was a lot easier for her mother.

Has a similar situation happened in your family? You talk long and hard with your daughter about behaving properly and she promises that tomorrow she will turn over a new leaf. She will make her bed, clean her room, wash, and brush her teeth without reminders. Off you go to bed, happily anticipating a new era of cooperation, only to rise and see that nothing has changed. The bed's not made, her room is still a mess, and she hasn't set foot in the bathroom. Your anger seems justified but if you look carefully you see that something is happening—your daughter is starting to change. Somewhere in her consciousness the thought has registered that it wouldn't be such a bad thing to honour the contract. She even tries to straighten up her bed. She might run out of steam, but it's a start. Notice these small changes and let your child know that you have noticed them.

The older an adult is, the less he welcomes unexpected surprises and the more he strives for peace and predictability, but to a child every day is new and exciting. The programme for development that is unwinding inside him prompts him to begin each day by testing the validity of old prohibitions and to search for new ways of doing the same old things. Routine is oppressive for the normal child, but for the orphan it is not so evident. He may not like the routine but he will dislike the parental pushing even more. Simply don't be in a hurry. Changes can take place in his consciousness but not appear immediately in behaviour.

A parent may not understand this and might try to direct the child's path of development, treating her as though she were disobedient or capricious, but there may be a spark of comprehension within your child. She may already have begun to make sense of your demands, realises she is wrong and promises to herself to behave better tomorrow. If you notice this spark, if you understand her on this subtle level of consciousness, then you should praise her first effort to improve. She will be grateful for your recognition, though she may conceal it, and will try even harder the next day to repeat the achievement.

If you reproach or discipline her again, the spark will go out. Nothing hurts more than injustice. Inside she had already decided to try to change for the better—it has just not yet become quite apparent in her behaviour. To a child, her plans and ideas—what is going on inside her head—are more real, more important than what is actually happening in the outer world. Thinking about something is almost the same as having done it, and what an insult it is that you haven't noticed! Your child might suffer your injustice with all of her strength while you carry on, insisting that she give in and tidy her room but she is far from feeling like tidying up her room now. Without tact on your part, the conflict may escalate from a slight misunderstanding to an utter disregard for adult authority, doubt in your sincerity, and even doubts about your love. If you continue to apply the pressure, the bubble might just burst with a bang, and cleaning her room will propagate more resentment than ever before.

As a rule, it is best to raise your child in the tradition of humanism. You can be firm but logical and predictable. With this approach, a child will develop respect for her parents and basic trust towards the world, and no great inner problems should arise.

10

Crises and Testing are Necessary for Growth

IS A CHILD ENTITLED NOT TO BELIEVE US?

Every child who has come to us from disadvantaged and damaging circumstances has resisted all attempts to change his concept of how the world works. Nothing in this new world in which he finds himself, be it a comfortable bed or caring parents, can tempt him to give up his values. It often seems that former waifs revel in the memories of their misfortunes and constantly test the resilience of this new world, wanting it to be real but at the same time wary of believing that it could be.

If you find it difficult to understand your children, take a look at the adults around you. A soldier returning from the front will continue looking around for enemies. Once deceived, a person may not trust anyone again. Another, having experienced power, will ruin his life for the sake of the illusion of holding sway over others. Is it surprising, then, that when you bring an undeveloped personality from one set of conditions to another, his behaviour or outlook does not change? His body may exist in his new, comfortable surroundings, but his memory, feelings, and even his power of reasoning, are still trapped in the past. He has lived through it and interpreted it in his own way and it is more real to him than the present you have suddenly created. Accustomed to not believing anyone as a condition for survival, your child will not believe in the new reality you have given him, so be prepared to be put to the test, and be glad of it. If it is successful, your child will be ready to accept the new rules of the game and the new world. In fact, you are less likely to witness similar changes in an adult, who also will cling to his delusions and refuse to accept a new version of reality.

DISTRUST

Many different theories have been advanced on how to overcome a child's distrust of adults. Here is one: why not suggest to your child a game of blind man's buff? Go into a forest or some other place where no one will see you and cover the child's eyes. In this game there are two roles: the 'leader' and the 'blind'. The leader is the strong and savvy adult and the blind is the child who, little by little, gets accustomed to relying more on the adult than on his own eyes. Then reverse the roles, with the adult playing the blind and the child playing the leader. This helps the child feel responsible for you. This game can be a very successful way of developing a child's sense of trust.

Another game that has become popular among western psychologists and that we use in Kitezh is called the trust fall. Stand the child on a table or high stool with his back to you. The whole family (or at least the mother and father) stands below in two rows, facing each other with arms intertwined. They then invite the child to fall backwards. You will observe how difficult it is for the child to overcome his fears and simply fall backward. If your child hesitates, be patient and tell him about a time in your own life when you had to overcome fear. Once your child achieves the trust fall, and overcomes the barrier to trust, the exhilaration is immense.

When you take a child in, you must be prepared to be flexible and patient. You must take the child for what he is and continually show him that he is entitled to your respect. You will need plenty of time to teach this wary little individual to share his feelings with you. You must learn to listen without judging, and avoid repeated lecturing. How many adults do we know that like criticism?

You will gradually have to teach the child to express his thoughts and wishes in words. Sometimes it is enough to simply describe the child's action, e.g. 'You smile when you look at this doll. It is beautiful and you like it.' or, 'This robot is cold and hard. It seems frightening and you frown.'

On a different level: 'Papa, Vitya said I was an idiot and we had a fight.' Reply: 'Do you feel hurt? I know how hurtful that can be. You don't believe him, though, do you? We all know you're not an idiot—even he knows it. It's just that for some reason he wanted to hurt you. What do you think? (This question helps transfer the child's reaction from an emotional level to a mental one.) And when you fought, how did you feel? Do you think perhaps now it's time to make up?'

There is no need to moralise or condemn. A child needs help in solving his problems, understanding his feelings, and expressing them in words. Gradually you will teach the child that talking to parents can bring relief from stressful situations and a feeling of security. Thus you will gain the right to the child's trust as he grows up.

EMOTIONS

When he was a little over three years old, Svyatoslav said good-bye to his favourite aunt, Lena, who had been staying with us in Kitezh for a few days. 'Svyatoslav, sweetheart, I'm leaving now. Give me a kiss.'

'No!' said Svyatoslav, turning away, 'you're leaving and I'm going to miss you.'

He refused to kiss his aunt, but one little tear rolled down his chubby cheek. All the adults who were present withheld their tears, but a child should not have to. Adults who work with children and who have problems, and particularly foster parents, must control how they display their own emotions. An emotional reaction can be utterly incomprehensible to a child, and more damaging than physical punishment. When a child is confronted with adult emotions she cannot understand, she can be frightened and confused. We are not saying that foster parents should not feel emotional; rather, they must make certain that the child understands their emotions.

If you are angry, your own children may not understand the cause of your anger. When they see angry parents they don't ask why; they simply try to escape or protect themselves, because anger is a very strong and dangerous emotion. This is why if you cannot avoid showing your anger, at least be careful to explain to your children why you are angry. Try to avoid giving them an image of guilt. Even if you are feeling angry with someone else, the child will take it as his fault and feel guilty. Do you remember how you felt when your parents argued in front of you? Did you not feel as though the whole world was collapsing? If a foster child happens to witness such a conflict, he will put up a wall in self-defence between himself and the rest of the world. This also applies to your own blood children.

In Kitezh, we have had a few cases of children who had parents but had the same psychological problems as orphans. And although such families may appear from the outside to be 'normal', they fail to promote the healthy all-round development of the child. This is not the fault of the parents. As a rule, it comes about as a result of lack of knowledge on their part.

DASHA'S STORY

Hers was a nice Moscow family. Her father had his own shop, her mother worked as a building engineer, and both loved their son and daughter.

Dasha: I was five and Sasha, my brother, was ten. Our parents left us at home alone one day and asked us to tidy up the flat but Sasha went outside to play with his friends. My parents came home and for some reason yelled at me. Then I remember the doorbell rang. Papa went to let Sasha in and there was so much shouting in the corridor. Papa had injured his hand and Sasha ran off again.

Dasha's mother: Our doctors advised us to send Dasha to a sanatorium for treatment. She was seven and very ill. I still have harsh words for those doctors. I don't know why they wouldn't let me visit my daughter. In a month they returned her to physical health but broke her psychologically.

Dasha: I remember the sanatorium. There were a lot of children there, and they were always fighting. After being there, I was scared of being left alone. When I got back home, I couldn't be separated from my parents, even when we were at friends. I used to cry a lot. They even bought me a dog so that I wouldn't be lonely. I used to dress the dog and train her. If I didn't have her next to me, I used to hug a cuddly toy. I was scared till I was twelve.

Just a month in the sanatorium had induced severe pain and fear in her. We have been trying to determine how this happened. Dasha, who was used to close contact with her parents, felt abandoned in the new surroundings of the sanatorium. She tried picking one nice woman from the staff with whom to form a special bond ('she would read books to me'), but every eight hours the staff on duty changed. A little person is simply not given the time or opportunity to develop a relationship of safe attachment when adults are coming and going. She is surrounded by other children who have their own problems—who are aggressive, demanding, and used to fighting over toys and the attention of the nurse. Our Dasha, who was used to another way of life, had become preoccupied with one worry: how to defend herself.

Eventually she got her hands on a big, soft doll. ('The doll made me feel better. I could think up any character for it, because I didn't have any friends.') From that moment on, she always dragged a soft toy around—her only warm, safe refuge.

Her father was used to being the head of the family and laying down the law. Her mother dealt with problems with her innate sense of humour. The children loved their parents, but too often they failed to understand the difference between one's commands and the other's jokes.

When he reached Year Eight in school (at about fourteen years old), Sasha stopped doing his school work and adopted the 'rapper' look: baggy trousers and a sleeveless vest. Constantly plugged into his Walkman, he stopped interacting with the outside world. Dasha also abandoned any attempt at doing her homework. Meanwhile, their father's shop was repossessed and he was bankrupted.

Such moments probably prompt people to contemplate the meaning of their existence. Their father paid up his debts and moved the family to Kitezh. He didn't try to pretend that he knew how best to help his children, but he turned to us. The children had no idea that they even needed help. In Kitezh, Dasha continued not facing up to her soft toy problem for another two years. At even the hint of a difficult situation, she would reach for the teddy and slip back into baby mode, starting to talk with a lisp, crawling on all fours or pretending to be a rabbit. In short, you couldn't get a grown-up response out of her.

This was a girl refusing to grow up, to step out of the cosy world of her past. We had to help her recognise that the world around her was completely real and, more importantly, a suitable place for her. We had to persuade her parents to abandon the joking tone in communicating with their daughter and start showing their genuine love in more traditional and transparent ways.

Her mother now had to sit with her for three hours a day while she did her homework, as well as reading books with her and having sincere discussions. Gradually, Dasha got used to the idea that she could talk to her parents not only in a playful 'fairy tale' kind of way, but also within an intellectual sphere. At our request the older children in Kitezh began to emphasise Dasha's 'grown-up-ness' when they talked to her. They demanded more sensible reactions from her and ignored her attempts to lapse back into babyhood.

Dasha would still protect herself wherever she could, sinking into her golden childhood, hiding behind toys and naivety, or pretending not to understand, but her peers continued to apply gentle but persistent pressure. Then her parents took into the family a foster daughter who was a year younger than Dasha. She had to show patience towards and be supportive of her new little sister and help her acclimatise to Kitezh. This increased her level of responsibility and raised her status among the Kitezh children.

Gradually, the communal approach bore results. Dasha grew more responsible; she began to work more consistently and to develop a talent for drawing. Then, something else went wrong. Her father died suddenly of a heart attack. The entire community waited with bated breath to see how Dasha would react to this shocking event but there was no regression. It confirmed for me the hypothesis that children, when allowed to develop according to their inner nature, will, without even knowing it, choose a healthier response.

This is what Dasha wrote in an essay a month after her painful loss:

If I was a magician, I would bring back my papa and make him never feel any pain. I would make my mama the most beautiful mama in the world. I would make it so that there weren't any hunters and I would look after the animals. I would make everyone in the world forget about their problems and delight in everything, even in little ducks and the sunrise. And I'd make all the children in Kitezh do well at school.

This did not mean that all her problems were solved but it does suggest that she had developed a new strength to deal with them. The following is a fragment from our conversation a year after her father's death:

Dimitry: Dasha, you're twelve now. Do you feel like you've changed a lot?

Dasha: Yes. Now I often dream about people. Before I used to just dream about the forest, and now I dream about people. And in real life I have to think now about what I say. I mean, I have to choose my words so that the grown-ups in Kitezh understand me. It's difficult.

Dimitry: Do you think that you've grown up?

Dasha: I've grown out of my dresses! And the boys have started to look at me differently. I have got older, but I don't feel very excited about it. I'm still scared.

This is a girl who has learned to look inside herself. At the very least, she now understands what is happening to her.

11

Peers: Help and an Alternative

What else influences a child's development? The 'law of the pack', for one. From the beginning of human evolution, the pressures of society have shaped the future of its members. Similarly, at the age of ten or eleven and particularly in the teens, peer group pressure is far more influential than any admonitions a parent might make. A seemingly insignificant factor, such as a friend's cynical judgment on a matter, can seriously affect the long-term influence parents can have. For most children, regardless of age, successful relationships with peers are more important than scholastic achievements and good relations with parents. In adolescence, the preoccupation with 'how do others see me?' is paramount. I will expand on this later.

How can a child from the street or children's home become sincere and open? Who can teach him to trust people and share his innermost secrets? How can he be confident that the good advice and emotional support of the family will really help? To a child, peer communication can feel like the blows of a club. They do not give each other a chance to relax. In the 'jungle', those who open up are doomed to perish. This model of behaviour is directly tied to survival. There is no time for subtle details and the need to understand and feel is largely ignored.

Children see the world in a completely different way to adults. Here is a quotation from an essay by a seventh-year student: 'Andrei is not a bad person, but he does like to pick a fight. That's why I don't like him . . . and he's kind (!). Also, I don't like him because when he picks a fight, I beat him up, and then he goes to find another friend.'

Many children cannot and do not try to understand the reasons for their actions. They are unable to analyse the actions of others or predict their reactions beyond those which are standard and often repeated. Emotional and intellectual communication becomes primitive, impoverishing their inner world and depriving the soul of food for growth and development.

But this is only half the problem. In a literature class, my students were unable to describe the hero of a book they had just read. They could barely describe the appearance of the character let alone the character's inner world. I was quite struck by this. It did not seem to be a question of literature, so I asked each member of the class to describe their neighbour to their other neighbour, who would then try to draw the child as described. Unfortunately, we cannot print the pictures here, so you will have to use your imagination.

The descriptions were as follows:

Vanya—he is big, he has a big nose and big lips, and long hair.

Yuri—he is tall and thin, he doesn't speak much, and he smiles.

Anton—he is cheerful, he hears everything.

After the initial shock, I spent three literature lessons teaching the children to look at each other, and then we learned the vocabulary with which to describe both our outer appearances and inner worlds. After that, their writing projects progressed much more smoothly. That was not the most important thing to me, however. I was much more delighted to see the new interest with which they started to look at each other.

In a children's home, children simply don't have the opportunity to learn the names of the various emotions around them or how to react to them properly. Many children never come across certain feelings, and when they do (in a film, for example), they don't have an opportunity to discuss them with adults, make sense of them, and file them away in their archive of experience. They are ignorant, therefore, of the meaning of many very simple words and actions. For such children, it is practically impossible to summon up an historical figure or a literary hero in thoughts and feelings. For normally adapted children this is a basic element of imaginative play.

When we identified this problem, we started to look for ways to change the internal programme in our children's perception of life. We saw that it was not a matter of force. Persuasion is useless. You cannot erase the old programme because the mind refuses to be left in a vacuum. We have to try to help our children see the laws at work in the world around us, to see how easy the world is to discover and to make sense of the mysteries around them.

At the Teachers' Council, we encouraged the parents among us to discuss each other's thoughts and actions with their children at teatime. Suddenly evenings in the family became a time of reflecting on and synthesising topics introduced in class. After a few months, this collective effort to become more aware of each other began to redirect the children's interest from the world around them to looking into themselves. This was a real success.

'Dima is trying to create a community where children and adults talk to each other on the same level, where everyone notices the world around them, not just to fight each other for a piece of bread. I think we're getting there!' This is what Andrei wrote in an essay. In the margins of the same essay he made a note for me of quite a different nature, 'I know that life is against me. I'm the unhappiest person in Kitezh.'

This was the most tangible success yet. Andrei had found the courage to share his real thoughts. He had managed to ask for help and support. He had assessed his strengths and achievements. Sometime around then, we started to have soulful discussions. I am not saying that life was suddenly filled with rainbow colours for him, but I do think that he grew up in that time and started to take responsibility for his behaviour. There would not have been such fast progress if we had not shown interest in talking to him.

He didn't know how much he could get from talking to adults and didn't believe it was possible. You have to create this habit gradually over the course of short conversations, each of which must stand independently and leave the child with a feeling of satisfaction. 'You got a high mark? How did the other children respond? What did your teacher say? Tell me more. How do you feel about it?' This kind of approach means our adults have to behave truly responsibly and in a well-thought-out way. Adults have to learn not only to guide children but also to open up the world to them and help them to realise their potential, find their vocation, and develop their talents and the skills necessary for life in our complicated contemporary society.

Even if it seems appropriate to make a remark or offer a constructive piece of criticism, hold back. It will not benefit you and can appear to the child as an unwanted intrusion into his private affairs. Let the habit of sharing news become grounded in your daily family routine. Let tea, sweets or jam become companions to these talks along with a feeling of peace, happiness and openness. Having started with neutral and therefore safe topics of conversation, you can gradually move on to more abstract issues, such as the future or moral topics. Initially, it ought to be the child who chooses the issue to be discussed.

A person cannot develop in his own way without feeling a connection with other people and with humanity as a whole. Talking from the soul to a trusted friend is the age-old basis of traditional psychotherapy. That is the hypothesis on which our work is based, but in practice things are much more complicated.

THE PROBLEMS OF OLDER CHILDREN

Fourteen-year-old Natasha is bright and very popular with the boys. In a moment of openness she said: 'Before we used to go for walks together and it was fun, but now I only go with the girls. Boys are so stupid.' This was an acknowledgement of her inability to understand people around her and to construct normal relationships with them. Take my word; the boys in Kitezh are not stupid. Natasha is unable to notice anything beyond their aggressive behaviour. Having seen the pain and bitterness in her parents' relationship she avoids deep relationships of her own. Both her parents and teachers have noticed that Natasha reads a lot in literature classes and focuses particularly on the relationships of the protagonists and the reasons for their actions and emotions. We came to the conclusion that this is the safest way for Natasha to develop her own reactions. Experience shows that by repeatedly working through fears in fantasy she will stop being afraid in real life.

During a psychological game the following dialogue took place between Tanya, thirteen, an intelligent girl with low self-confidence, and Sasha, fourteen, an intelligent and aggressive boy who is a poor student with no friends.

'Tanya, do you feel safe around Sasha?'

'No, not at school and not here,' (she half smiles)…'I am afraid of him.'

'Sasha, Tanya doesn't feel at ease around you, could you try to make her feel more comfortable?'

'How?'

'Say something nice to her, pay her a compliment.'

'Err…' [he blushes and lowers his gaze]….'well, I…. No, I can't.'

'You normally swear at her, so now just praise her instead. Say "Tanya, you are so…" '

'No, I can't.'

Sasha, as tall as an adult, jumps up, starts to cry, and runs out of the room.

Here is a composite portrait of a senior pupil: he is rude, begrudging of kind words, and disinclined to be sincere with his parents and yet expectant of courtesy from them and respect for his freedom. He avoids taking responsibility, refuses to take part in amateur dramatics, denies he is gifted, yet at the same time constantly strums the guitar. Revolutionary in their words, his songs are scornful of the values of the older generation. This hides the fact that he is unwilling to take risks, challenge his weaknesses, take responsibility and show concern.

The deepest life crises are often experienced during adolescence. Childhood comes to an end and the time to mature has arrived. Three changes take place simultaneously: rapid physical growth and sexual maturation, preoccupation with how others see them, and the search for life's meaning and one's destiny and place in society. All unresolved problems come to the surface, but now they must be resolved consciously and with free choice. The healthy, mature character has qualities such as faith in the world, initiative, independence, and aspiration to be master of one's own destiny. In these cases, teenagers solve their own problems in the light of parental advice. If, however, they lack self-confidence and inner strength, they will find it hard to speak to parents, despite the fact that they need them more than ever. Parents must demonstrate care and concern; they must help the child accept his problems and learn to deal with them without destroying his self-confidence.

A common mistake made by parents: a boy comes home from school troubled by several problems. Consciously or not, he is looking for compassion and support from his parents. His mother is having tea with friends and says to him, in offhanded humour: 'You look a mess. Look at the state of you' (or something similar). She doesn't want to hurt him, but her attention is with entertaining her guests. The teenager, however, is on a completely different emotional wavelength. These sorts of jokes are evidence of his parents' thoughtless attitude towards his troubles, and the presence of guests only increases his feelings of estrangement. The main point is that at fifteen, no one likes to be the object of an adult's jokes or jibes. It is humiliating. As a result of this kind of unintentional slight, loving and caring parents could lose contact with their teenage child during this important stage of development.

Children's subcultures exist regardless of the will of adults and are to all intents and purposes outside adult control. They can be very dangerous—a powerful educational influence that can change a child's outlook on the world, his values, his identity and his behaviour. One challenge in raising children well is how to show them which subculture is suitable and which is not. How do we, as adults, determine which one is suitable?

We have quite a simple solution to this problem. Parents must encourage their teenagers to find friends who will understand our programme and influence them in a desirable way. My mother liked to arrange small parties for my school friends and even my girl friends. These parties gave her a chance to get to know my friends and thus participate in building my new vision of the world. In Kitezh we have a unique opportunity to organise the interaction of all the children within the community. We find the most intelligent and cooperative individuals who with our help become the leaders. Five years ago these leaders officially organised themselves in the Small Council, like a mirror of the Council that runs the community.

The Kitezh Children's Council is a group of older children who are elected by all the children. It helps our children learn how to choose their own leaders from among their peers. These act as mentors to the other children, allocate jobs in the community, and award 'compensations' for misdeeds. It took about a year for the first group to overcome the fear of responsibility and apply themselves to the duties of leadership. Where did this fear come from? From a fear of testing their own strengths and finding they cannot do something, and from a fear of knowing themselves—understanding their emotions, impulses, memories, abilities, potential resources and purpose.

PARENTS' PROFESSIONALISM

How do we understand the professional approach to child rearing? We bear in mind the aphorism of the ancient Greeks: 'everything flows, everything changes.'

We tend to regard everyone as constant, stable and unchanging. A child is not constant. He changes all the time and sometimes his past is more relevant than his present. A girl in the fifth year starts to suck her thumb and speak with a lisp because she is afraid of a new and challenging exercise. The teacher speaks to her in language appropriate for mature students. He becomes angry and the girl regresses deeper into the safe infant age of incomprehension and irresponsibility.

When a child does something wrong, it is an ideal opportunity for us to give a concrete lesson and draw conclusions. Each life situation is a lesson. Take a child of school age: say only nice things to him, feed him, and allow him to sleep as much as he wants. Will he be motivated to develop? Will he strive for anything or have any desires beyond his immediate and basic gratification? Probably not. In supposedly ideal conditions people do not develop, they stagnate.

The openness to acquiring knowledge from all possible sources occurs only when the child is very young. In later stages, absorbing new knowledge and information becomes more difficult as the child strives for peace and the least amount of effort. Any noticeable transformation seems to come through conflict, crisis and even stress.

Crisis is a necessary condition for development. Like any vitamin, however, it should be taken in limited quantities. Inner conflict is inevitable when a young personality gets more and more information about life and has to release his previous primitive image of the world. It is always painful to change one's way of understanding the world.

Be aware that the more emotional you are, the more it affects the child. Therefore, if your child is fighting in the street you should control your anger. Emotion will cloud your thinking and obstruct your efforts. Remember, it is the child who should feel the emotions, not you. Your main task is to discern how you can use each given circumstance to teach the child. The choice of this lesson is yours. I repeat once more: it is your choice because each case is different.

INSUBORDINATION

Parental love is the main condition for a newborn baby's survival. Without a mother's love, without the altruism and the self-sacrifice of parents, a baby will die. The capacity to love is a gift from God and of immeasurable importance in the survival of individuals and mankind as a whole.

Equally indispensable is the 'instinct of insubordination'—the principle mechanism of evolution: the main guarantor of the progressive development of humanity.

In children as young as two, we have noticed that insubordination is a dominant feature of their behaviour. It is a rejection of parental authority, a desire to do exactly the opposite of what is expected and an indifference to painful consequences. This can be seen within a broad framework—from a readiness to say 'no' to any parental suggestion to absolute obstinacy that leads the child to climb over the banisters and then fall to the floor, to touch fire, and to jump over puddles. Parents react to this in a traditional manner; they prohibit this and that in an attempt to protect their beloved child from harm and their favourite vase or tablecloth from inevitable ruin.

I once spent an hour writing down every word said by a young mother to her child in their home. Ninety per cent of the words used were forbidding commands: 'Don't go there. Don't touch. Don't shout.' If a child followed all these commands he or she would become a flawless plank of wood standing somewhere in the corner not bothering adults. If the adult is constantly strict and assertive, all initiative will be taken from the child.

The most logical approach is to fill a child's life with challenges. Give him complex toys to test him and give him a place where he can run wild. Nature cannot be deceived in this way. Within a few days a child will get used to this space and will desire to move beyond it. The instinct that insists on ignoring restrictions and pushing the borders of proscribed behaviour to the limit will always take a child out of your control.

My son never had a lack of toys or space to play and yet each morning he insisted on climbing on top of a wobbly pumpkin to reach some small insignificant bottles high up on the top shelf. What attracted him was their inaccessibility. I can say without exaggeration that it was the most dangerous place in the house. It obviously stirred within him the same feelings that make mountaineers risk their lives to conquer mountain peaks.

The significance of insubordination becomes clear time and time again as children reject demands and exceed set boundaries. This can be annoying for us because we make every effort to influence our children to be obedient for their own good. Perhaps it is some kind of a divine joke to make life difficult for parents by instilling in their children a passion for insubordination!

The environment imposes a totally different pattern of behaviour. From the Stone Age, the whole system of humanity's education was built on the foundations of obedience—a beating with a branch, edicts and regulations, laws and courts, and so on. To survive, a person must submit and become one of the crowd. Only the primal instinct of insubordination overcomes laziness, indifference, and the willingness to become just another obedient sheep.

A fool breaks the sombre mood of a king, heretics disturb the monolithic character of a religion, and it was Columbus who destroyed the idea that there was nothing beyond the horizon. Without the desire to exceed boundaries, there would be no science, no art, and no creativity.

This is why God (atheists can use the term 'nature' instead) regards the 'emotion of protest' as the most important. The urge to rebel, a fundamental dissatisfaction with what we already have, is an unconditional reflex.

As teachers can we allow ourselves to ignore this important quality of development, this mechanism of evolution hidden deep within the human being that is also a great source of energy? The fact that this energy can be directed towards destruction even of self does not mean we should refuse to use it. We can expect the harmonious development of the personality only if a teacher's efforts cooperate with evolution.

Rejection of limits and boundaries yields scientists, discoverers, successful businessmen, as well as those who seek to disrupt public order. The quality of insubordination has no moral characteristics. It is neither good nor bad. Thus it challenges the skilful teacher to divert this energy to creative effect.

There was a situation when two boys of fifteen, Tom and Pasha, were in conflict with the community and their parents because they had decided that they were already grown up and had the right not to do homework and to drink and smoke like 'real men'. They decided to have a barbecue. It is against our rules for children to light fires unsupervised but is the divine right of teenagers to break the rules and seek the limits of their social environment.

Nevertheless, adults must preserve the rules. We arranged an educational meeting in which we chided the barbecue organisers. Surprisingly both offenders were bold enough to explain that we adults are not ideal ourselves and didn't always act according to the rules. Of course, some of us were offended, but if we just punished the young lads for insolence without any sympathy, the result would be just one more offence to their souls.

We let them go for a time, and tried to discuss the situation and express our concerns to their friends. There were a few days of heated discussions amongst the children about who was wrong and who was right and how you should behave towards adults. Finally, we persuaded the most active leaders that adults also have the right not to be ideal, but an adult is still an adult, someone who earns money, protects and teaches; so while you are in Kitezh you must respect the adults and live according the their rules.

12

Kitezh's Therapeutic Model:
Some Issues to Ponder

In Russia, a child living in an orphanage is under the care of the state until he or she reaches the age of eighteen. Only five per cent of children in the orphanage system are real orphans. The other ninety-five per cent are what we call 'social orphans'. They have at least one living parent and have been removed from parental care because of severe abuse, most often as the result of alcoholism. After eighteen, the state is only obliged to provide some form of accommodation for real orphans, usually in the village where the child originated. Social orphans have no provision made for them at this vulnerable stage of their lives. Having lived in an institution for many years, they are obliged to return to the families who abandoned them in the first place, or to find their way in the world unsupported and unaided.

Why is it that the communal way of life continues to offer the best environment conducive to positive development? Why has it been impossible to create such an environment in a children's home? To understand why this is the case, it is important to recognise that as our culture develops, popular perceptions shift, and consequently there is a change in the generally accepted view about how best to bring up children. The new era does not require us to churn out bland, law-abiding citizens who are simply components of a society based on mass production and some ideological construct. When we provide children with an education, a family upbringing, and therapeutic treatment, our ultimate aim is to allow them to discover their true calling and to facilitate the process of self-realisation within a rapidly developing culture. It is also the case that a social system based on a communal way of life requires a person consciously to make decisions about what is right and wrong.

Children's homes have now fallen out of favour in many countries. It is only in Russia that, with a misdirected persistence, we continue to place all children without parental care in state institutions. Moreover, it is illegal to separate siblings, and therefore everyone is treated in exactly the same way; no distinction is made between those who have talent and those who are incapable of much development, or between those who love to read and those who have already turned to crime and drink. The system does not treat people as individuals, yet no two children are the same.

Is evil contagious? Even relatively well-adjusted children will undergo a change for the worse if they are in the hostile company of formerly homeless children. Some people might think this view is insensitive, but what is insensitive is the attitude of officials who fail to take responsibility for placing children in institutions according to their need. The same approach should be applied to children as is applied to adults who are ill: children should be treated as individuals.

We, the foster parents of the Kitezh therapeutic community, support the negative view of institutional children's homes expressed in the Stockholm Declaration 2003 (Second International Conference 'Children in Residential Care' held in Stockholm), but we cannot agree with its conclusion that the only acceptable approach to the normal raising and development of children is the foster family. This does not mean, however, that we favour the proliferation of children's homes.

If the care system for homeless children in Russia were to be based entirely on fostering and adoption, would the foster or adoptive family be equipped to cope with all of the challenges involved? Our experience of working with foster families in the Kaluga Region shows that this form of care has its own shortcomings. Functioning in isolation, and without the support of a well-developed social structure, the foster family cannot cope with all the problems that arise. Too much depends on external factors—the environment in which the family lives, the school the children attend, the friends the children make locally, and the extent to which the foster parents understand basic psychology.

In Great Britain, it is now regarded as axiomatic that it is best for children to be brought up by their own families or, in the case of children in care, by foster families. Sadly, fifteen years of experience with biological and foster parents has convinced us that by no means does every biological family provide a child with a better upbringing than that provided by a children's home. Not every family, however normal it may appear, will help a child develop into a well-rounded individual and equip him to live a normal life. A children's home still allows a young person a certain freedom (albeit the freedom of the jungle), which I regard as a better environment than a family that either regards their child as a possession or simply treats him with disinterest.

In countries with solid democratic traditions, family values and wider social values tend to go hand in hand. The child hears the same messages at school and home, on the street and on TV. In countries that are going through political and social reform, as Russia is, there often is no common agreement on what is morally acceptable, not to mention common attitudes towards social rights and a citizen's duties. In the twentieth century, Russian people suffered four traumatic social upheavals, the scale and psychological effects of which may be difficult to grasp by the western reader. The first was the elimination of the Tsar, the aristocratic class, and God. The second was when Stalin executed or exiled the romantic Bolsheviks who had staged the revolution and repressed the intelligentsia who asked questions. The third was when Khrushchev told the people that Stalin was not the Father of Humanity, but was himself a criminal. The fourth was the *perestroika* period under Gorbachev, followed by the inauguration of capitalism by Yeltsin, who told the people that their lives had been devoted to the wrong ideals.

In such circumstances, adults don't feel confident enough to explain to children what is good and what is bad and for what kind of future they should prepare. TV and mass culture instilled the dream that amassing wealth can make a person happy and people bought into it. Now, twenty years after *perestroika*, many people are questioning if this is enough. Thus, children don't know what to believe and who to believe. There is a saying here in Russia: 'Optimists learn English; pessimists learn Chinese; and realists buy a Kalashnikov.' Children who are without parental protection in these turbulent conditions are under even greater stress, exacerbated by society's lack of clear pointers as to 'what is good and what is bad'. Physically transferring the child from an unsafe family to a marginally safer one will do nothing to alter his or her perception of the world.

If a child is to come to terms with being abandoned, he needs not only a psychologist (of which there are not enough in Russia), but also foster parents who have themselves received special training in certain aspects of psychology. The development of a well-rounded individual is a complex and multifaceted process. As the child's inner development programme 'runs', it is simultaneously programmed by his environment. The child will, in a free and largely unpredictable way, draw information, indeed his whole life experience, from his environment. While a child is growing up, he is influenced by a million unpredictable environmental factors that often defy rational analysis.

For there to be a happy outcome, an orphan must be provided with a holistic world that can stimulate his development in accordance with his instincts; provide for his effective rehabilitation and adaptation; and ultimately accelerate the pace of his development. This is what can provide the starting point for therapeutic treatment.

It goes without saying that the work required exceeds that which can be accomplished by a family alone. As children assimilate from all available sources the information that either confirms or refutes their new experience, it is imperative to coordinate the efforts of the family, teachers, medical professionals and everyone else who has contact with an orphan child. This is why we believe that a therapeutic community offers by far the best solution to the problem of housing, educating and nurturing orphan children.

The therapeutic community is a living, complex organism that is constantly growing and changing and in which all the organs are constantly interacting with each other and with the outer world. Anyone who wishes to become involved in this organic process must follow his every thought and action and be aware of his personal pride, the desire to take and not to give, and the impulse to change others instead of himself. Society is a pre-determined framework that will accept only those additions that are moulded to fit its rigid structures. In Russia, a person's development is determined not by divine will or by one's personal ambitions, but by pressure from peers or the social surroundings. The inner laws of self-realisation will do their work within, but personal development will be hindered if the person is surrounded by a hostile environment. This is how a nonconformist becomes neurotic, alcoholic and a misfit.

Paradoxically, the very challenges we face are an emotional testing ground and are the best stimulus to development. Our surroundings must pose active challenges to provoke responses and to train our reason, our muscles and our will. Living in idle comfort robs a person of his will to develop and improve. The general conclusion we can make is that the most effective environment for development is one with well-defined rules that pose challenges while allowing children freedom of choice.

Success can be only be achieved by building an integrated world around the child, a world capable of stimulating free development in accordance with his natural potential, that will ensure the effective rehabilitation, adaptation and 'catch up' or accelerated development of orphaned children.

Foster families in Russia often lack the necessary training and the intellectual and material wherewithal. An important point is that the child is influenced not so much by the family as by friends and neighbours. Children reaching the age of adolescence generally cease to pay attention to their foster parents. Russia at the moment lacks a system of psychological support for youngsters leaving children's homes or foster families. The state ensures that they have a roof over their heads, but they often lose this and are unable to find employment because they have no model of how to live a decent life as an adult.

The youngster who returns to his neighbourhood and former house, with all the memories intact, where the neighbours expect the traditional patterns of behaviour, will be dragged back into his former patterns of behaviour. For example, you will offend your host if you don't drink with him.

The goal of the therapeutic environment is to restore in children a sense of safety and confidence in their abilities and show them how to achieve success. As the Kitezh experience shows, by finding knowledge and confidence, these children will be able to face the challenges of adult life adequately. For them to grow and gain in strength and experience, they must first be immersed in the special conditions that are present in the Kitezh therapeutic community.

THE COMMUNITY

Is it really possible to build a therapeutic community when society as a whole reveals, more and more, humanity's undying penchant for egotism?

For more than fifteen years, we haven't stopped working and we haven't lost our ability to analyse ourselves and our organisation critically. Every new stage of our development forces us to reassess our previous approach as we see our mistakes, analyse them, and try to rectify them. People are always people and the laws they adopt will never be perfect. The important thing is that they are appropriate at the time and they allow people to improve themselves and their relations with others and keep open their perspective for development.

What kind of people can live in a therapeutic community anyway? In our country, burned as it is by a bureaucratic version of social justice, which was the communist ideal, communities are not very popular. Maslow, however, asserts that, 'given certain conditions, the interests of society and those of the individual can coincide to such a degree that they cease to contrast and become synonymous'.

Humanistic psychology recognises the tendency in people, capable of self-realisation, to combine egotism and selflessness into some kind of higher quality. They do not push each other out of the picture, nor do they suffocate each other. In this ideal, developing environment, the work becomes a game. Vocation and profession becomes the same thing. The boundaries between the external and the internal, between 'me' and 'everyone else', fade away and personal development becomes a mutual, interactive process.

A community as we define it—a cooperative of honest and intelligent people intentionally living according to the rules of common sense—is not only possible, but also very good for your health.

Nowadays, this choice is becoming rare. To adapt to our constantly changing reality, people tend to avoid the profundities of human existence. 'The less you know, the better you sleep', says Russian folk wisdom. 'Don't stick out', or 'Keep your head out of the clouds'. If you avoid the deep questions, and don't find time for contemplation of the meaning of life, love of your neighbours and the good of humanity, you'll be much better at solving the real issues of survival. Just as in the jungle: if you are sidetracked or relaxed, you put yourself in a dangerous position. By behaving in this way, 'new' Russians are missing a lot. The truth is that the profundities of human life are the source of our happiness—our ability, as Maslow writes, to play, love, laugh, and, most importantly, be creative.

AMBITION IS TREATMENT IN ITSELF

Maslow writes, 'Trying to live without a system of values is psychopathogenic. Human beings need a system of coordinates to live and achieve, they need a philosophy of life... almost as much as they need sunlight, calcium, and love.' Loss of life values, as well as moral degeneration and cynicism, is a psychological illness that can result in physical illness. The worst crime against a child can be seen as any attempt on the part of an adult to destroy a child's faith in the good and humane world and in the justice and love that surrounds him.

An adult, presented with a far-off goal, consciously or unconsciously understands that to achieve it he will have to make a certain amount of effort and develop certain qualities. Setting ambitions and conceiving a way to achieve is a process that transforms all of us.

We try to help our children set accessible goals, as we know that it will subject them to transformation. The main thing is to help them see their goal, to believe in their ability to achieve it, and then let nature do the rest. Remember, though, that it can only be their goal that can lead to their self-realisation. Do not rush them or push them along; give them a chance to make sense of things, do things at their own pace, and make their own mistakes. If your child breaks down under the pressure of your will, then whatever marks he gets in a test, for example, he will turn out unsuccessful in the future.

We all feel the temptation to give our children 'a little nudge' to raise the demands made on them, to set rotas or make them behave, but if that were all we did, what kind of people would be leaving Kitezh?

The authoritarian method of child raising denies any possibility of alternatives or any doubts. It has no place for inner searches and certainly does not allow children the right to look within themselves. I would assert, however, that an authoritative approach need not necessarily be spiteful. This method of child-raising can be kind and affectionate, and yet offer no alternative ways of thinking, destroys initiative, prevents them from making mistakes, so they do not develop the strength to correct unavoidable mistakes in the future.

If we beat our children into giving us the answers we want, we are not teaching them to think independently. If we feed them and give them all the essentials without any effort on their part, or without allowing them any choice in the matter, we rob them of the opportunity to answer for themselves and to work for a reward.

The ideal environment must be full of challenges. Any challenge entails a risk. In our society, a risk for a child tends to pose a problem and create a risk for the adult who is responsible for the child. If there is no risk at all, however, it is impossible to raise a strong and healthy individual.

13

The Art of Soulful Parenting

CHALLENGES IN THE SURROUNDING ENVIRONMENT:
A STIMULUS FOR DEVELOPMENT

Kitezh is a consciously created developing environment, the main aim of which is to help children to realise their full potential through a series of obstacles and challenges appropriate to their personal development. We do not try to creep into the subconscious of our children. Rather, we carefully design our environment, taking into consideration that each child takes from his surroundings whatever best meets his needs. By following the progress and personal development of each child, we are able to add to each child's surroundings certain ingredients and impose tasks, while we help him work through his problems, strengthen his will and make discoveries.

In Kitezh, for example, children themselves set themselves targets or goals. Those can include doing their homework on their own, helping mother with the housework, or spending more time talking to other children and adults. During the week, every day, the child marks off on a list whether or not the goal has been achieved. At the end of the week, the child informs his classmates of the progress made. In this way, he or she learns to overcome weaknesses and to make an effort. In addition, children are taken off to take part in longer field trips, and to put on plays in which each child tries out the main role. We do not raise children, rather they grow up of their own accord: this is self-realisation. Strength should flow and find its own direction, while gathering pace and confidence.

We try to work with such concepts as 'the meaning of life', each person's 'vocation', the meaning of 'happiness', and 'self-realisation'. But how can we encourage a child to embrace new experiences of this kind? In the system we have created, certain psychological and sociological factors are designed to interact and strengthen each other to boost each child's strength from within.

Everyday life in the community should provide a constant stimulus to activity and orientate our children towards making decisions while deterring them from settling into stereotypical patterns of behaviour. Otherwise, after a child has got over his initial surprise and becomes accustomed to how his new world works, he may start to economise his efforts, reduce his activity to a minimum, and expend all effort on sustaining his own comfort. Instead of exercise, he would seek to sleep longer; instead of reading, he may find a way to play on the computer; instead of drawing, it would be television. The responsibility of the adults in Kitezh is to pre-empt this tendency and present the children with new boundaries to overcome. In this way, and this way alone, is it possible to stop the intellect from stagnating.

MAKING CHANGES TO THE INNER PROGRAMME:
OLGA'S STORY

I remember being at my grandmother's when I ate a whole bowl of soup for the first time. I was really difficult to feed. When I was little, they had to make four different breakfasts for me. I had a lot of things when I was little, but I never had enough. My first real memory is when I was five or six. We had gone to live in Germany then. I had loads of toys and sweets. Mama always bought fruit for me; there wasn't anything she didn't let me have. I was a happy child. Mama never shouted at me. I was the centre of her world.

Father treated her really badly, but he would put the whole world at my feet. He even wrote me letters in rhyme, with lines like, 'my beautiful daughter, my swift-footed doe.' But I hated it. He would come home and start singing praise to me but I would be sick of it. My elder brothers didn't get that from him. Father would beat them if they didn't do well at school. I probably sensed the problems between my parents and was instinctively on my mother's side because I had always been closer to her.

Then they had a big argument in Orel. Mama found out that he had a girlfriend. He was saying he was going to go and live with his girlfriend in Siberia. They were on a bridge and Papa picked me up and took me with him. I was shouting that I wanted my mother. They stayed together and we moved to a village near Tver where the air was really fresh. But my parents carried on arguing. Of course, they tried to hide it from me.

In school I was a scaredy-cat. In the first year I got the lowest mark and I felt so ashamed. I decided it was never going to happen again and I started to work hard. The most important thing for me was always to get a good mark so that I would be praised (I felt valued). Gradually I developed a thirst for knowledge. By Year Eight or Nine, I didn't even have to make any special effort. I was the president of the school students' council and I could always do my homework very quickly, so I had lots of time for other things outside school.

When Mama was about to have Nastya, her second husband left her. Then I realised that I would have to help. I was nearly eleven when Nastya was born. Mama was on her way to work and I was carrying the shopping. She started shouting at me, saying I didn't do anything to help at home, that I just made a mess with all my toys. I was looking at my shadow, forcing myself to think about her. I knew she only had me for support. I realised that we were alone all of a sudden and that I would have to change. I knew then I had to help her. I had to go and fetch water from the fountain and stoke the fire. We had a really basic life. I had to manage our money and go and ask for things at the shop. I was suddenly swamped in this adult life. We were alone.

I had to run out of school to get home. I never went anywhere. I wasn't interested in going to school discos anymore. I used to run home to Nastya. I was the odd one out in the class. My friends found it a bit weird but they still came to see me. Once, Papa came back to see Mama and they started fighting. I had to run for the police that time.

Nastya could have died if I hadn't helped out. She was so tiny and I would sit with her and read her stories. I loved spending time with her. It gave me such a warm feeling that there was this little person by me who needed me. She was mine to look after. I think of her in the same way now. She's the best thing that I've got.

When I came to Kitezh I was fifteen, I realised that I wasn't at home here. If I had to do something, I carried it through to the end. The other kids were very wary of me. They would go and drink tea together and keep away from me. It wasn't so simple. I realised that I had to try harder to make friends. I made friends with the younger kids. Just as in the village, we used to hang out in the garden and we were nicknamed Tigger and Co. I started to act in the way that I was happy with. The first six months were quite fragile for me. The boys in my class didn't notice me. The idea of Kitezh finally got through to me in the autumn, when we were out picking valerian roots and you told me about the knights of King Arthur and Merlin. That really touched me. I was fascinated.

Then you started to invite me for breakfast and started to teach me to analyse things. With you I could take things to pieces. You were the only one I felt safe talking to about everything and I started being able to philosophise.

Dimitry: Why did you not feel able to talk freely with other adults?

I could, but not in the same way. You invite people to talk and you notice what they're thinking. When I'm talking to you I feel like I am important to you at that time. You don't get sidetracked from the conversation. I was getting used to what I was allowed to say and think. You ask questions and wait for a response, and anything is allowed. Other adults seem too busy with their own problems. It's harder to talk to them. And I don't like gossip. It is just talking without analysing facts, and talking about people is like judging them—'she said something stupid' or 'she was dressed stupidly'. I don't understand why people talk like that about each other.

The most important thing for me is working with children. I love it. I love it when they hug me. I really felt this for the first time when I realised the most important thing is that the kids trust you. One girl asked me to be her godmother…then she lived with me for three days when her parents went away. Do you remember when Masha ran in the snow, hysterical, with no coat on, and she started screaming that no one loved her? I told her, 'I love you.' And she listened to me. Then I asked her if she loved me and said, 'if you do, then come back indoors.' And she came back indoors straight away. That was really important for me. That was when I really started to make sense of things.

All my experience of raising children in Kitezh convinces me that a normal child has to be able to make mistakes and that the direction of his or her free choice will be directed towards goodness and development and not towards stagnation or degradation. If an adult is faced with a dilemma, if he is overcome by feelings of insecurity, or loses faith in himself, there is much less chance of persuading him to make a choice in favour of satisfying his curiosity. Out of insecurity an adult may abandon some opportunity if a negative or painful experience has led him to lose confidence in himself. If I researched this phenomenon of choice only in adults suffering neuroses, then I would hardly be able to accept that there could be another direction of human development, and I might not even believe that people could be healed.

But as unlikely as it might seem, we have one child after another whom, in the process of growing up, throws off the burden of childhood memory, tears down the walls of distrust, leaves the past in the past, and develops the courage not only to move forward himself but also to help others. Helping others, incidentally, might be one of the key factors in the process of self-recognition and self-therapy.

For millions of years, the instinct of adult love has been the main guarantee of the survival of newborn babies. Without a mother's love, without the altruism and self-sacrifice that is genetically inherent to parents, a baby would be sentenced to certain death. Similarly, the ability to love is not only a truly divine gift but also the primary condition for survival of every human creature and for humankind as a species.

We are all familiar with the type of brooding hen mother who fusses over her children from the very moment of birth. Doctors in natal units have long noted that excessive nervousness on the part of the mother is transferred to the baby, who doesn't understand, but feels the emotion within it nevertheless.

Recently, newspapers reported that the granddaughter of the Greek millionaire Onassis had inherited his wealth. Nevertheless, who can really envy her? She couldn't walk until she was three because her mother instructed her nurse to carry her for fear her precious daughter would fall over.

For some reason, many parents think that love gives them the right to be tyrants over their children and control their every step. This love is a distortion, based on egotism and the idea of people as property. Only pure, selfless love can save your child and keep him or her free from fear and complexes. Such love has no ulterior motives, is without jealousy, or expectation of profit. It allows parents to be proud of their children's success without ascribing that success to themselves. Such love allows a child to be himself and creates the best possible conditions for his unhindered development.

The approach taken by humanistic psychology fully agrees with the spiritual point of view. It would be naïve, of course, to expect a professional psychotherapist to love all his patients with his whole heart. This sort of love, however, is expected of all parents, including foster parents.

According to Maslow, basic love shapes the recipient. The recipient of the love develops an image of himself in relation to it; it allows him to make peace with himself and feel that he is worthy of love. This creates the essential preconditions for his further development. The question is: can a human being develop at all without this love?

The Russian Orthodox priest, Anthony Surozhskii has written that the absolute condition of love is openness, which, ideally, should be requited, but sometimes the openness is characteristic of only one party. Being open means being vulnerable. Everyone is vulnerable to being heartbroken, when neither bitterness nor hatred makes up for the pain. You should forgive and forget, because spite, betrayal, misunderstanding and lies are transient things, whereas we are around for a lifetime. The ability to carry this faith to the very end and to love with all your heart, only so that the recipient of your love can grow to fulfill the extent of his potential, is nothing short of heroic.

At birth, a child is inherently frank and open. She is not familiar with pain, cruelty, or treachery. Disappointment, however, is quick to follow. The first meeting with pain will leave a deep mark on the psyche for the rest of her life. The child's concludes, 'I was an open person and then I learned a painful lesson. Now, I will never allow myself to be hurt in that way again.'

We are not just talking about the children. You as a caring adult must make the effort of being open. Your child reads the laws of the world around him in you. The more open you are, the more information he can receive. This means, however, that you sacrifice the personal right to spontaneous reactions like anger, resentment, and emotional outbursts resulting from sheer exhaustion.

Analyse yourself. If you can calmly observe your child's behaviour changing slightly every day, despite your natural desire for stability and consistency, and if you can retain good humour even when your beloved offspring behaves 'badly' from your point of view, your love is working well. If you can enjoy the process without expecting certain results; if you accept your child's right to make mistakes; if you do not lay claim to your child's ideas and feelings but try just to understand and help, then your love is just right.

This approach is justified from both a spiritual and a moral point of view and from a therapeutic point of view. It opens up a greater opportunity to understand your child. For if you love a person, then you will concentrate less on your feelings than on his. A Russian proverb 'In the soul of another is darkness' (i.e. it cannot be seen) tells us not to look inside ourselves. The same Russian folk wisdom asserts that the face is the mirror of the soul. A child's soul is open and can be read by any loving parent.

For a child's psychological wounds to heal, something has to penetrate the psyche and compel it to recognise that reality has changed. The child must psychologically accept his new freedom and his endless, unconditional importance for someone else. This process is effectively equal to a miracle. Humanity long ago called this strength, the love that can teach and heal.

NIKOLAI'S STORY: A THERAPEUTIC CRISIS PROVOKES A CHANGE IN THE VALUE SYSTEM

When we received Nikolai from the orphanage, he was six years old. He had a very limited range of emotional expression. He was able to continue a dialogue using the right words about the need to learn and make friends, but in reality, it was his fears and hesitations about adults that were speaking. He really was afraid and this was his way of hiding. He was timid and sweet like a little puppy-dog, but he was really a tortoise inside his hard shell, believing nobody. I suppose that he himself reasoned that was the best way to behave. He was used to seeing the world as a place where everyone is an unpredictable enemy. The limits of his abilities were written with pain in his consciousness. His alcoholic parents and the older boys in the home hammered into his consciousness the principle of survival: 'Don't try anything, don't be seen or you will be beaten'. These principles, which had helped him survive, were in his blood from the first days of being in the orphanage when he was about a year old; thus, he is unaware of them and they are inaccessible to his conscious mind.

How can we liberate his consciousness from this fear and pain? He needs energy for transformation. If he has no energy he cannot change and embrace a new vision of the world; and without the vision he will have no idea where to put this energy. We usually understand energy as a need, desire, or intention. So how can we make Nikolai feel a great need for change? If everything around him is comfortable and easy and he becomes sure of himself, he will acquire enough energy for transformation; but no one wants to change when life is comfortable.

How can we put the 'dream', the possibility of something better, inside someone's head? 'The dream' is not an image; it is the state of bliss, experienced in very early childhood that includes the feeling of security, warmth, love, freedom, achievement and victory, and unconditional joy. This is the state of being of early childhood. This dream is a feeling. Later, we search for the material forms that we imagine will return us to this bliss—money, status, power, etc.—but we are unaware that we are searching for a feeling, not a tangible possession. Only later, when we have tried these material substitutes, do we begin to question the path.

So how do we plant the idea that something is worth the effort of change? We must find the energy within the child to help him to construct a realistic dream. To change the programme of a young person requires showing him, with some practical examples in his life, the closest way to this bliss. We present him with opportunities to achieve something through his own efforts. In Nikolai's case, this was to make a box in woodworking class. He received praise for good work; he received money when we bought the box, and he has a sense of achievement that he did something, and did it well. In this way he was encouraged to come out of his shell and explore a little of the world around him. His previous programme was challenged. It is important to say all this experience is very practical and very personal so he cannot argue with it. He personally can now form his new vision of the world.

Nikolai stole money with the heroic intention of supporting

his colleagues and winning new friends. While Nikolai was reluctant to admit his wrongdoing, he also knew that if he admitted stealing money, he would be accepted by his friends, respected by his elders, and loved by the adults. It had been a year since he had come to understand the value of having friends, in being part of a group, and loved by the adults. In his former life he had no friends.

For me the idea of penetrating a child's psyche, or soul, is a concrete and tangible one. There must be something that causes the heart to beat faster, a warm rush that leaves one person and touches another whose heart beats nearby. It is like a stream uniting the two souls, giving both a feeling of peace, trust, and unusual closeness.

This quality is usually referred to as empathy or identifying oneself with another. In the Orient, the phenomenon of identification with another is well known and occurs in various philosophical traditions. It is the ability of human consciousness to deeply penetrate the feelings and thoughts of another. It is fascinating to note that it is a quality innate to children from birth.

The American poet, Walt Whitman might not have been familiar with oriental philosophy, but he understood the concept of identification:

There was a child went forth every day;
And the first object he look'd upon, that object he became;
And that object became part of him for the day, or a certain
part of the day, or for many years, or stretching cycles of
*years.**

Many monks, elders, and sages in Russia and other cultures are gifted with a sagacious intuition and are able to relate immediately to the soul of anyone who comes to them for help.

Perhaps this is the only reliable way of understanding and helping a child. Scientific research is useful, provided it does not become dogma that opens the path to papers and dissertations but closes the path to truth.

Long ago, the editor of the Russian magazine, *The Young Communist Leader* told me, 'I know how best to raise children. I studied pedagogy at the university.' I genuinely hope this man has grown wiser since then, or at least has changed his profession or not tried to raise children.

My experience with children and parents has shown that practically every mother has the talent for empathising with her child's feelings. Almost every mother is inherently able to shut her mind to everyday matters and concentrate on the more subtle issues around her. We could give this ability many names—contemplation, identification, embodiment—but whatever we call it, we refer to a changed state. This experience gives a person a rush of new strength—a feeling of joy and purpose in the world. In addition, recognition of transient strength gives impetus to recovery and strengthens one's faith in oneself.

Identification doesn't only help parents understand their child; it also helps the child experience his surroundings more astutely and truthfully. The ability to contemplate with the heart, as they say in Japan, provides a child with a powerful source of happiness that chases away fear and inner doubts. 'Beauty makes the world a better place', Dostoevsky asserted. Recognising and experiencing beauty is a form of therapy in itself. You can draw a teenager's attention to the beauty hidden in the depths of his psyche and teach him to value his own senses, higher thoughts, and motives for action. In this way you will give him an instrument with which he can solve his own psychological problems: a key to the inner world.

The unfolding beauty of a sunset, a heartfelt prayer, some

especially strong emotion, or a wave of inspiration are all experiences which touch the very foundations of a child's view of the world and remind him of his uniqueness. Maslow likens this feeling to a visit to one's personal heaven from which we then return to Earth full of memories of heaven. Anyone who has experienced a moment of rapture or inspiration knows that at that moment, the personality compromises its defensive position and releases itself from restrictive control. The child's awareness is broadened and given a rush of strength, of joy in life, and love of the world. Such moments are attributed in all cultures to a range of higher human values. They can have a considerable impact in therapy.

It is just this kind of experience that can wipe the slate clean of a negative world view in a child's consciousness. Such experiences should be maximum strength and emotionally charged; they should have the irrefutable flavour of a personal life experience and in intensity of colour they should exceed the grey, everyday routine that weighs upon the child's psyche. We have hundreds, perhaps thousands, of witnesses to the fact that the creative enlightenment of such heightened experiences has real therapeutic effect.

All our children take part in theatrical productions. They make their own costumes and scenery. One of our girls, Eva, came to us from the orphanage when she was thirteen. She was the product of a rural orphanage, with a simple vocabulary and strong emotions, which she used as weapons. We took a risk giving her the main role in George Bernard Shaw's play, *St Joan*, but in this vehicle, her 'drawbacks' suddenly acquired the quality of nobility—of a woman knight. Joan is not only a fighter but also a woman who shows the most subtle of feminine feeling: gentleness and tender love. In her performance, Eva felt these for the first time in her life and was applauded vigorously by the audience. For some time after the production was over, she felt that she was still in the role. For the first time in her life, she realised that she could move and speak beautifully, act nobly—attributes she had never experienced before—and that she could be respected by others for displaying them.

Have you ever tried to talk to a child, who has lived through a tragedy, about his past? Children in such circumstances often turn momentarily into stuttering fools, struggling for words. Their whole being resists the retrieval of these memories: bringing back an event from the past means bringing back all the pain, shame, and fear attached to it. Therefore, before teaching a child to look inside himself, we need to help him triumph over his fear and grow stronger.

The way I see it, the source of strength lies somewhere in the child's soul. It is like the Russian fairy tale that tells of two streams—one with living water, and one with dead. The latter is composed of personal memory, subconsciousness and bears fear, while the former is the collective memory that contains heroic mythology. Jung called these two areas archetypes because they exist in everyone. We are all familiar with some myths and the mighty feats they contain. The challenge is how to help a child psychologically learn from them. Myths, like many fairy tales, are often tragic—they simply reflect the real laws of life—but they summon us to action and heroic feats.

I once heard about mothers who avoided reading their children frightening fairy tales. Their children grew up not knowing about the wolf that ate the grandmother, were never scared by the trolls and witches, and never empathised with the seven goat kids. Everything they should have reflected on, at a tender age, was hidden from them, and as a result, they did not overcome their fears. The Russian child-raising specialist, Nikitin, said it is dangerous to live in sterile surroundings; a child should get muddy occasionally and get covered in scratches and bruises so that his immune system learns to fight the microbes he comes into contact with. The same is true of the child's ability to immunise against fear.

The child's surroundings also have a role to play. The wolf had to eat granny, but if a granny were to be eaten in real life before a child's eyes, then we would really have a case needing therapeutic intervention. Fear makes people tense up; it distracts their attention, robs them of the ability to take initiative, and prompts them to grow a thick shell. A shell is still a shell; it protects the weaker inner being from outer reality, but it also constricts the growth of the person it envelops and slows down personal development at a basic level. In school, the child finds it difficult to be decisive, to build relationships with his surroundings, to sit still during lessons, and to share cultural values.

The most surprising thing is how many adults have grown a second shell to protect them from their inner fears and taboos. As we have noted, many people find it impossible to look reflectively inside themselves. Often, such a person will wind up with a personality that is squashed from both sides like the filling of a cheeseburger, and his ultimate fate is not much better. You need strength to build your fate. Where are you going to get it from if not from within yourself? But what if your inner world has been a cordoned-off territory for many years, a taboo; a haven for demons of the past? This is why parents must, first of all, help their children make peace with themselves, especially with their pasts, so that they don't feel compelled to grow an inner shell. Just this one step can allow the personality to inch onward towards healthy development.

14

The Challenge to Change

MORE OF PHILLIP'S STORY

At the age of twelve, Phillip is weak and a bit slow for his age. He has become an expert on objects and natural phenomena but when it comes to personal relationships he is deeply unhappy. He is unsure that we can help him.

For the last five years, he has always insisted on fairness and fought for his rights. He always passes blame on to others, making enemies within five minutes. He will get into a fight over a seat on a bench, he lies habitually, and he is quick to wriggle his way out of reading or doing his homework. His whole experience in Kitezh seems to support the fact that you can't break the rules without getting in trouble and your lies are always found out, yet Phillip responds impulsively, in the moment, without thinking of the consequences of his actions and without making note of his experience for next time. He's very good at carrying out instructions like 'bring me some wood' and 'can you help me do the washing up?' but he's incapable of anything involving effort over an extended period or of working independently without being watched over. When he is alone, he is unable or unwilling to sit down and do his homework, even though he knows well the trouble he will get into if he doesn't.

Phillip is also rude and provocative towards his big brother Alexey, who is four years older and three times stronger than

Phillip. Alexey's reaction has been to beat up his brother. Still Phillip continues with his provocation, as if he didn't see the connection between his behaviour and the beating. When people were developing their instincts in their early history, the individual who failed to see reality did not survive. In our time, civilisation allows even those who are blind to dangers in human society to survive.

The primitive hunter creeps through the jungle. Suddenly, from out of the bushes in front of him, leaps a huge beast with gaping jaws and flashing teeth. The curious observer who stopped to look before acting would not survive. Thus the unconscious reaction to any danger was developed and passed down through evolution. Of course the world has changed since the time of the hunters. We don't need to fight to survive in the world of nature; instead we are faced with the world of society. Mistakenly assess your situation, say something with the wrong nuance, at the wrong time, and you could seriously compromise your relationships. Social mishaps can ruin a person. Phillip reacts to anyone older and bigger than he is as to a potential threat. That reaction is so instinctive that he cannot contain it or control it consciously. The experience of being beaten yesterday cannot alter the pattern of his behaviour today. To cut a long story short, we have been able to help Phillip. As he grew older, he learned to perceive the relationships between people and to control his reactions. This happened towards the end of his time at school, when both his teachers and classmates made a deliberate effort to show him where he was going wrong and helped to alter his behaviour.

In the Russian fairytale of Baba Yaga, an innocently mistaken reply to one of Baba Yaga's riddles puts the hero, Prince Ivan, at risk of an untimely death. If Ivan cannot solve the riddle or carry out a challenge, he will lose his head. Similarly, in our society, a careless slip in front of your boss could mean losing your job, your wife, and your family. Even that is nothing compared to the fate of thousands fifty years ago in the Soviet Union who were sentenced to the Gulag or even to death for behaving wrongly at a party meeting or telling an untimely joke overheard by the wrong person. Through millions of petty squabbles and conflicts, the rules of model behaviour are beaten into us by society. If we see trees in front of us, we walk around them. In the world of social relationships, children often try to 'flatten out the bumps' without seeing the sharp corners and brick walls that the social world contains. Learning to understand the subtleties of interpersonal communication is a painful process.

Here is an excerpt from one of my Citizenship and Society lessons in Year Seven:

Phillip, please, will you run up to the wall and hit your head on it? Why not? Do you think it will hurt? How do you know that? Oh, you just know, do you? You learned this simple truth when you were a baby. You learned not to run up against walls. You don't run into trees when you're walking in the forest. You've learned to avoid ditches and the corners of houses. So why haven't you learned not to run into Alexey? He threatened to punch you again today. So why do you start one fight after another? You don't have the right, nor are you strong enough to exert your rights violently. Why do you not notice the ditches and obstacles in your relations with other people? Do you think there is just air between you, or a vacuum? Well, we all have to interact in the same complex field, where all of us have the same rights and responsibilities. We have expectations and agreements with each other. If Sasha tries to sit down and take Vasya's place, of course Vasya's going to protest. If Vasya tries to steal Andrei's apple, of course Andrei will threaten to do something to him. How could you think there is a vacuum between you? There are walls and barriers between you. You have to forge precarious footpaths through the dense forest between you but you don't notice and that's why you come up against aggression and violence.

You are all blind and need to ask Baba Yaga for her magic wand. Let her magic guide you. Or, if not magic, then at least look up on a map to find the minefields, dangerous precipices and rickety bridges around you. You need a map to make sense of your surroundings.

So you've left home with your map and on your map is written, 'Don't be late for school, or there'll be trouble.' There's no point in having a punch-up with the kids you meet on the way; it's as stupid as running in front of cars or throwing things at shop windows. At school, you find that everyone has instructions written on them about how to behave with them. You see Alexey? He's a big guy and stronger than you. It's written on him, 'Don't touch me or you'll get it'.

Nevertheless, Phillip still tries to irritate him and start trouble. He has a map, but he screwed it up, shoved it in his back pocket and forgot about it. Now he's running around in the jungle—he kicks a lion here, treads on a snake over there, oops, then he runs into a cannibal tribe—he is cheeky to the elder, sticks a finger up at the chief hunter and shouts that he wants to share the hunters' winnings. Well, the tribe kills him. What use was he? In Kitezh you can make mistakes like those without such dire consequences. In the jungle with the cannibal tribes, you can't. The reward for a mistake is death.

If the cannibals only beat him up, he would curse God and mankind and say that the world is evil and so is everyone around him. In fact, he carries the evil inside himself; he carries his own poison within him. He is blind and doesn't see the dividing lines or the precipitous paths between people. You have to create a bridge with a smile, or stretch out a hand to ford the river, but

Phillip will insist on running headlong against the walls in front of him and refuses to understand. He hasn't learned to read the signs that people use to mark dangerous places and he doesn't know how to ask the way. Why? Because he thinks he knows the right way. He does everything without questioning himself. When he gets a knock on the head, rather than ask, 'why?' he shouts that it's not fair. But when he learns how to learn, to accept advice from wise men and serpents on his way, then he'll find the treasure of Vasilii the Great. Then they will call him 'Prince Ivan.'

What can you do with children who cannot or will not analyse the reasons for other people's actions and who cannot predict their reactions? The whole wealth of emotional and intellectual communication boils down to a primitive scheme that impoverishes the inner world and starves the soul of growth and development.

Our response is to try to develop their intellect while they are still growing. The first stage is to teach them to use their reason. The second stage to encourage them to independently identify, analyse and work through problems logically. Here's a vivid example:

MARA'S STORY: BREAKING THROUGH THE BARRIERS

Mara came to us from an orphanage for 'retarded' children. She took a long time to learn to read and succeeded with the untiring support of her parents and teachers, but she had little awareness of herself and her surroundings. She scarcely saw that there were inner connections between people; she didn't sense the subtle threads governing relationships and behaviour. Around her was a vacuum, and she behaved accordingly.

She used to cause havoc in class, pestering the others in Years Five and Six. She threw tantrums if she thought her teacher's judgments were unfair and ran out of the room banging the door behind her. Her new mother took valerian for headaches and would pray to God to bring her daughter just a little peace and reason. Neither of these, however, was perceptible in her character; in their place she had plenty of energy. In Year Seven, her spare energy, which wasn't spent on intellectual concerns, was directed into her physical growth. She wore size forty-two shoes and had grown taller than the girls in Year Eight. Soon, her growth spurt was followed by a change in her voice and an emotional surge.

Now, at thirteen she is quite grown up and you might think she was sixteen, but the tantrums she throws are those of a five-year-old. If life presents her with the slightest challenge that seems impossible to her, she becomes a toddler without any capacity for logical thought. Instantly, the virtues of moderation and dialogue are forgotten, all memory of previous family rows are reduced to nothing, all promises to be good and grown up are thrown out of the window. The toddler takes control in her infantile way but where has she acquired this model of behaviour? Most probably from her mother, whom she observed in drunken brawls with her fellow drinkers.

I saw the following scene with my own eyes. Mara was walking with her friend, singing some kind of jolly song about summer. They met a couple of friends, in whose company there were some boys. Her behaviour instantly changed.

Both thirteen-year-olds started using words and intonation that they could only have picked up from the most unsavoury company. (It is unpleasant even to write about it). They were eight when they came to us. We had worked a great deal with them on etiquette and manners and even introduced them to prayer. We thought that they had learned to behave nicely, as we had hoped. We had forgotten, however, to teach them how to behave with the opposite sex (or rather, had shied away from it, thinking it too early) and they did not know how to deal with the situation. Instead, from the depths of memory a ready-made example was dragged out of the archives. Imagine what horrors are there if her mother, with an alcoholic tendency, was a representative of the world's oldest profession? Add to that her two or three years in children's homes. Judging by this, she took in the largest volume of information at five, and much of that was emerging now, like some irrepressible part of her worldview. Of course, we cannot disregard the influence of contemporary films and pop music: the crude offensive with gaudy lips and eyes, maximum flesh on show and provocative behaviour.

'Hey, bitch, your belly's hanging out; your trousers are way too baggy…'

'Shut up, you cow, I just wanted to see if that wimp noticed…' [There are boys around. These lines are all acted out for them!]

An older girl's comment—'Do you really think you can act like that?'—only increases the crude behaviour.

This is a manifestation of the deep competitive instinct. It blossoms like a luxuriant flower an hour later at the disco, then is accompanied by tears and hysterics:

'Bitch, why did you touch Alexey? He's mine!'

'You bitch yourself; you're the one flirting with Nick!'

The question is how to replace this low level of the consciousness with a model of behaviour that is more socially acceptable. The concept of 'correct' behaviour in the company of boys is so deeply ingrained in the consciousness of these thirteen-year-old girls that an innocent attempt on the part of the older students to persuade them to stop it will be given a hostile reception. Should we lay down laws? Sometimes it is necessary, but forbidding something does not mean it is forgotten or erased; it will happen later and a prohibition will suppress joy in life and potential self-realisation. In effect, it encourages children to repeat the mistakes of their parents.

This stream of thought leads us to the idea that children have ready-made roles that they find difficult to throw off. We might deduce the presence of some kind of predetermination, but that is a rather primitive point of view. The subconscious, to which Freud devoted so much attention, must be more than merely a repository for suppressed instincts. Nobody has yet shown that the path to the subconscious is closed or that it cannot change.

In September, the Teachers' Council established that Mara, bored by her immature peers, had started to take control and had become a little dictator. Her bullying could slow down her peers' development. Her unbridled temperament was an obstacle to the atmosphere in class. For her sake and that of her classmates, we decided to move her up a couple of classes, into Year Nine. It was unofficial, but then our school is small enough to be flexible. The kids in the older class were bigger and more confident so Mara could no longer be so bossy. Someone expressed concern about the possible psychological trauma she might go through in being moved: 'She'll be upset about being made aware of her inadequacy' was the rationale. Nevertheless, considering her disregard for others' opinions, her energy and her potential, most of us were hoping for the best. I remarked, 'Mara has been getting Ds for two years in her year group. Will it harm her confidence if she still gets Ds in Year Nine? Hardly. It should be a boost to her confidence to be in a higher group, and it should increase her interest in studying.' I was hoping for a miracle.

From time to time miracles happen because the process of human development remains unpredictable. This was the conversation at the Teachers' Council six months later.

'Mara got a C in her algebra test.' [She attempted three out of five questions.]

'She is lagging behind a bit in history. She doesn't quite understand the subtle differences between different ethnic groups.'

'Mara is having difficulty with trigonometry. She wants to be able to do it, I think, to keep her face in front of the boys, but she's still not quite determined enough.'

In other words, within six months, Mara had turned into quite a different person. She had started to focus on her work and on raising her status in the group. She had struck up a new friendship, with Marina from Year Ten. The results seem to merit expression in professional language—something like, 'Promoting the subject by two levels of difficulty has enabled her to use more of her energy resources and provided a comprehensive solution to the question of her personal development.' In other words, her environment had forced her to stretch herself. We need to step up the challenge in such a way that the children agree to it.

We had a role play game for the whole of Kitezh. All the children were divided into teams. Competition makes the passions boil. The participants were learning to work for the common cause and stand up for common interests. Mara was designated as the leader of her team. She was serious, determined and focused and she played her role honestly. But then Sasha, thirteen, refused to do the washing up when she told him to. A row ensued. 'You idiot! Do you want a punch?'

Mara was not capable of solving conflicts in an adult way and so at the first signs of an impasse she resorted to her infantile behaviour. She didn't understand subtleties in negotiations with her peers. This boy suddenly became a mortal enemy and the only way to deal with enemies is to punch them, so Mara punched him. She was surrounded by the community and they tried to stop her and talk some sense into her by talking to her like an adult. She was in five-year-old mode. She felt insulted and therefore justified in resorting to her image of the world where her view of absolute fairness reigns as in fairy tales.

Gradually she got used to people trying to persuade her to do something different. In the children's home she would have been sent to the corner as punishment, but in the relative safety of our community, Mara forgot herself and played the five-year-old. This is where mentors come in. One of them, Ivan, pulled her aside. 'You know you're destroying the team, you're messing things up.'

'So what? I'm sick of your stupid game. I don't like it anyway. I want to stay at home on my own.'

'We can't let you. You have to apologise to Sasha for hitting him.'

'I'm not apologising. He's an idiot; he wouldn't listen to me and I was only doing what I was supposed to as the leader.'

'All of us in the team think you were wrong.'

'I don't care.'

'Don't you care what people think of you?'

'Why should I care what they think?'

Ivan loses his patience at this point and gets cross himself. 'Well, if you don't go and apologise to Sasha within five minutes, we'll kick you out of the game and then we'll go to the Youth Council to decide whether you can stay in Kitezh.'

This is where the five-year-old in her becomes gripped by fear and she crumbles to make way for the more sensible and constructive thirteen-year-old. Until then she has been playing in a fairy tale. Fairy tales are heaven for children, after all. They can make up their own rules of fairness and justice and do what they like—order others around and shout, etc.

Ivan made her understand that it is enough playing and that she's faced not with an obedient Prince Ivan but with a fire-breathing dragon. Her team mates are no longer fairies and gnomes as she might imagine, but brick walls that she can bang her head against as much as she likes but they won't let her back into the fairy-tale world. In this stressful situation, her mind started working at full power and Mara realised that now she really had to leave the fairy tale for the real world, where no one is going to give her a second chance. The grown-up Mara knows that. She stopped her hysterics, wiped dry her tears, apologised and made peace. Thus she began to learn how to identify safe harbours and dangerous reefs in her relations with other people. It is interesting to note that often even the cleverest students cannot identify them.

KATYA'S STORY

Katya's story illustrates how difficult it can be to access and reform the inner programme and how parents can be deceived by outward appearances. There are many instances of 'successful' people in the 'normal' world who are driven to success by fear of failure or exposure; a belief that they only exist according to what they have achieved and that they will be 'found wanting' at the last judgment.

Like Phillip, she would die for 'fairness' in the form that she understood it. In Year Ten, she argued until blue in the face that I wasn't teaching history properly. She was gifted with an excellent memory and was diligent and accurate in her work. It was not a problem with grades. She was just sure that her image of the world was the right one. If something contradicted her point of view, she fought to defend it. This had led to many problems with her teachers when she was in a children's home, before coming to Kitezh. She enjoyed a certain respect with us.

Outside of my lessons, she was exceptionally polite and obedient with grown-ups and would always complete her homework on time. It would have been fine if we had not been getting the impression that the motive for her behaviour was fear. She was afraid of being less than excellent all the time. She was afraid of any aspect of her thoughts and feelings being challenged, which she perceived as threatening to her. She didn't allow anyone entry into her emotions, not even herself. She laughed little and with difficulty but cried a lot, albeit not in a childish way. She never discussed either her laughter or her tears with anyone. She didn't have any real friends. She didn't engage in a dialogue or an exchange of opinions. She simply told adults what she thought without seeking a reply. Any kind of dialogue was too complicated a form of interaction and would involve allowing someone too much access to her inner world—exactly what she feared. She simply knew what was right and would allow no compromise. She was lonely, but it was better to be lonely than to try to change herself so she didn't try to change.

After all, do adults lie to themselves to any less extent? Throughout their lives, they complain to themselves about how awful their work is, where they live, etc., but they don't do much to change either themselves or their outlook on the world. Rather, they do everything they can to teach their 'right' way of thinking and their understanding of the rules of life to their offspring. Thus they teach their children to be just as unsuccessful and as unhappy as themselves.

It was only when she turned eighteen that Katya told one of the girls (whom she would be able at a stretch to call her friend) about how, when she was little, her father used to beat her and threaten her with a knife, and that her mother had been a prostitute. That was why she never trusted men or women. On top of that, she knew that other children in Kitezh had gone through similar traumas and they seemed happy and hopeful, so she saw reason not to trust them either. There was no use trying to persuade her otherwise: she was simply too certain of her convictions. It was this quality that helped her be the best student. It was a sad paradox, though, that getting the best marks served as a defence behind which she could avoid evaluating herself and deflect negative comments. The everyday level of consciousness by which she oriented herself was flawless. She was terrified to look beyond that and into herself and admit her fear of her surroundings. Getting As and being well behaved let her feel relatively safe. I wouldn't care to say whether the same would be true in other places, but in Kitezh she was cosy and safe, which meant there was no reason to change. We didn't anticipate that we would have to help her and so we didn't present her with big enough challenges.

PASHA'S STORY

Pasha came to us from a Moscow family, not of his own will. His parents brought him to Kitezh when he was in Year Nine, saying that 'he doesn't study, he simply doesn't care about it, yet his teachers love him all the same'.

Up until this point, his life was certainly comfortable. He warmed the hearts of our unsophisticated teenagers with tales of skateboarding, inexhaustible supplies of beer, and the unlimited freedom of the city dweller. He was a perfectly average D-grade student who went by the nickname of 'Detzel' (meaning 'titch' and not intended as a compliment). Pasha's authority, based on his imaginative tales, started to wear thin after a couple of months, when their repetition started to bore the majority. By that time, however, Pasha had started to feel the security of Kitezh. Here, no one called him 'Detzel' or sent him off to buy beer. Here, he was valued by adults and children for his help with chopping logs and writing poetry. Our teachers were outstanding in their patience, but at this age boys aren't interested in empty, unearned praise; it's patronising to them. The teachers pitied Pasha, but he wanted them either to be exasperated or delighted with him.

It must be said, in Pasha's defence, that he really was ready to fight to improve his status. He just was not used to studying and didn't have much inner discipline. Then he put himself under external pressure: he decided to go and live with another family. This is accepted in Kitezh. Sometimes, old psychological ties to the parents inhibit free development. There are things that we happily excuse in others but do not allow our own children. For these reasons, we let Pasha move to another family where he felt a greater sense of empathy and where he was creatively stimulated but not indulged.

He was told it was time he got a bit stronger. He wanted to, but was afraid of showing it for fear of disappointing himself. At the same time, the new, non-frightening but still strong adults were talking to him about having to grow up and be strong and independent. Pasha felt all this. He felt they respected him and had great hopes for him (which is true of all our children). He started to express his creativity—first, by painting murals on the walls of some of Kitezh's houses, then by getting involved in the community's Internet newspaper. Every day he was dragged, literally, to martial arts training. In Kitezh, the training has the psychological objective of nurturing courage and confidence. The training, which we call kung fu, given that it is inspired by the oriental ritual of this art form, is immensely popular, especially for its element of mystery. A year after Pasha arrived in Kitezh, he suddenly managed to overcome his fear in a one-on-one combat situation with a visiting student. He didn't beat his opponent, but, true to the philosophy of oriental martial arts, he did triumph over himself; he overcame his fear and was clearly excited about it. I saw it myself, and even though I had hoped it would happen, I was still surprised and delighted.

It was interesting to observe how Pasha extended his newfound courage. He named himself editor of our Kitezh newspaper and adopted the pseudonym Hazard. He finally started studying seriously. He was not suddenly at the top of his class—he had missed too much in Moscow—but he set himself the goal of becoming a journalist and knuckled down to study the subjects he would need to pass to get into the university. He studied in the same way he had fought in his kung fu duel: he was abrupt and emotionally involved; he would rise to great heights of optimism, only to tumble to depths of hopelessness or despair.

Imagine how difficult it was for the Teachers' Council to follow all his ups and downs. We talked at length about whether we could depend on him to organise a musical evening or work with the younger children; whether he should get a low mark as motivation; or whether to avoid giving him any crises to cope with and let him evaluate his success himself. Pasha's parents listened carefully to the recommendations made at the Teachers' Council and did everything they could to carry them out.

Six months later, Pasha was elected to the Children's Council unanimously, and soon thereafter started to assist with teaching history to the Years Eight and Nine classes and Russian to Year Six. Most importantly, he stopped harking back to his past in Moscow and started to see that his happiness now depended on personal achievements and not on his geographic whereabouts. Happily, after two years in Kitezh, he started to realise his creative and leadership potential.

Kitezh proved to be the favourable surroundings that allowed his metamorphosis but there was one essential precondition for success: he needed to be prepared to give up his identity as Detzel and to adopt a more adult one. He already had the talented journalist and the authoritative leader within him. He needed to transform his world view and see that the best way to fulfill his potential and satisfy his need for love and appreciation was through his own efforts. The role of the adults was merely to explain the rules of the game, as it were, and to provide the first impetus. The rest was done by Pasha's healthy, inquisitive nature with its inherent will to develop.

All of these stories lead us to two main conclusions:

1. A child's individual programme for personal development unravels in certain circumstances.

2. It is the social environment that either encourages shoots to sprout and develop further or breaks the little plant off at the roots.

15

The Kitezh Community Reaps what it Sows

EVIL IS INFECTIOUS, BUT SO ARE GOODNESS
AND CULTURAL BELONGING

When we first started our community, it took a long time before
the children who had joined us began to believe that the adults
weren't lying to them. Eventually, they started passing on their
confidence in our trustworthiness to the next generations of
children, facilitating the acclimitisation process.

By observing the necessary conditions of honesty and
sincerity, the adults and older students, in the role of mentors,
have been able to create a particular emotional sphere of mutual
support and understanding. The mental and emotional unity
that comes from open and honest discussion and from daily
interaction infects everyone, immersing them in the group
process and helping them to enjoy the unique experience of
trust, self-discovery and support from those around them. And
so, little by little, the common sphere of trust has become an
integral part of our common cultural ethic. That in itself was a
great leap forward.

At first, we had to rely on our strength of character to get the
children to do things like washing the dishes or not swearing at
each other. We had to explain to them the point of sitting
around a campfire together singing songs or watching films. A
real turning point for Kitezh came at the close of 2001 and early

2002. Until then, no matter what activities we suggested, there were always two or three of the older kids who would mumble, 'that sucks', or 'no way', and other crude expressions for 'that's a lousy idea', and 'I don't want to'. The younger kids would hear them and join them.

Sometimes even the adults misunderstood the meaning of the word 'community' and started to oppose what they perceived as our leadership's effort to treat as special those children who worked hard and tried to build positive relationships with the adults. They saw the success of these children as a threat to the other, less forthcoming, children. It got to the point where some were advising the achievers to behave more simply and not think about adult issues. What were they supposed to think about, then—what clothes to dress Barbie in, or new ways to get high?

Then—gradually, almost imperceptibly—the collective consciousness of our children began to change for the better. To this day, we still are not precisely sure what prompted the change, although some factors clearly contributed. First, our adults had grown used to each other and had developed a harmonious culture. The children began to see themselves as living within certain clear boundaries and to understand what was expected of them. Second, we had finally learned how to cooperate with each other at the Teachers' Council meetings, and this produced tangible improvements in our processes and procedures. For example, the Council inaugurated a daily timetable of the children's activities, from the time they rose in the morning until their after-supper free time, and started monitoring the daily achievements and challenges of each child, creating a balance in his or her schedule between periods of strenuous activity and concentration and of creative rest. The daily schedule of classes and extracurricular activities, the system of rewards and consequences added up to make the world of the community more comprehensible and structured for the children.

The older children started to become our allies. This was manifested above all in their willingness to listen to one another and agree on mutual action. Now, adult suggestions were not only heard by the young contingent, they were acted upon. The level of trust grew so much that the older children began to believe they could discuss their problems with some of the adults.

ROLE PLAYING, OTHERWISE KNOWN AS LIFE

The most natural state for children is playing. Play allows young people to live, vicariously but safely, through several full, emotionally rich lives in order to activate their many innate, latent talents. Our job is to provide the children with an opportunity to try out many varied roles and guises in order to expand the spheres in which they can behave confidently.

We adults can regard everything we do as work, and even cloak it in serious, therapeutic terminology, but everything should be kept within the mainstream of life. It is while playing that the stream of life flows especially strongly and happily.

THE YOUTH COUNCIL:
THE YOUNG SHOOTS OF DEMOCRACY

The following are excerpts from my notebook of August 2001:

We have noticed that the kids listen more to their group leaders than they do to adults, so we suggested to them that they move over to autonomous government. In citizenship lessons, the Year Eleven and Twelve classes have been discussing the voting system in contemporary Russia, have weighed its advantages and disadvantages and considered the advantages of democracy. Afterwards, the older students themselves worked out a role-playing game based on elections to a governing council. All the schoolchildren in Kitezh from Year Six upwards took part.

Preparations for the election demonstrated above all the absolute ignorance among the other year groups of the meaning and purpose of an elected council. To be honest, we were shocked, given that the community has been governed by an elected council for ten years. The kids had seen how the adults ran the meetings and voted on decisions. Seeing, however, is not the same as understanding. What we took for granted was completely beyond the experience of our charges. Therefore, it had never occurred to them to contemplate something that we had included in our community governing process for many years already. So, the first youth democratic elections in Kitezh's history took place amidst the utter lack of interest of the majority of the electorate. The kids had no idea what was going on or why it was in their interests. But, somehow or other, the council was elected and started to govern. Olga, Masha, Pasha and Feodor were elected to it by the children's vote.

It was difficult for me to explain to the kids that they were now their own bosses and that the grown-ups were no longer free to interfere in their activities directly. We gave the Youth Council the right to decide the children's work assignments, to collect homework in lieu of the adult teachers, and to organise holidays and birthday celebrations, with the Community Council providing finances for these activities. For refusal to participate in community activities or for violations of the disciplinary rules, the members of the Youth Council were given the right to ask for compensation to the community (e.g. extra jobs in the kitchen, cleaning, work on the farm, etc.).

Kitezh

From March 2002 diary entry:

Crisis: the older children have discovered that governing the others is no simple task. Life has forced them to develop new personal qualities. The relationships within the young contingent have started to get more complicated. They have started to ask quite heatedly and profoundly, 'Who are you to boss me around?' 'What should we do with those who don't obey?' 'Why not introduce a dictatorship?' Both children and adults have found a rich new topic of conversation and the adults have more free time as the Youth Council has taken over the responsibility for organising and checking homework, the housework and cleaning assignments, and so on.

At first, the Youth Council consisted of four people. Then almost all the students in the older classes began to get involved in its work. It began to be seen as prestigious to take responsibility over one or another sphere of activity.

I remember how, when I was at school, I avoided any kind of public responsibility until chance and a clever class leader made me director of the school theatre. But I never saw school in any shape or form as a home. School was, sadly, associated in my mind with pressure and violence. Kitezh is a home for our kids, in which they are in charge of their collective fate. But they understood this only when they were given the right to make decisions about what they can do in their home. Of course, everyone is different and the level of responsibility that each one wants to take on is different. It's a question of the dynamics of everyone's personal development.

The most important conclusion I've made is this: only when the children are convinced that something in life really depends on their opinions and efforts will they grow up and become more responsible. So it would seem that raising children effectively is a matter of giving them the power to decide for themselves. They can only understand adult problems and adopt adult values when they take a conscious role in adult life. Of course, there is always an element of risk in this process, but children must have the right to make mistakes. We learned just in time that if we want to have dependable allies and colleagues, we cannot have a monopoly on power and we cannot think that adults are always right just because they are adult.

From November 2002 diary entry:

It's interesting that even when the cleverest children take on responsibility, they don't immediately escape the cunning traps they are lured into. It's only when they discover what a burden power is that some of them start to sigh with nostalgia for their previous lack of responsibility. But despite their sighs, having become obedient performers in the grown-up game, none of them wanted to return to childhood. By watching their older peers, the younger children are starting to change. Now, if they don't have a public role, it's seen almost as a sign of mistrust or inadequacy.

For a long time, the adults have been trying to persuade Mara to take part in a theatrical production. The more forcefully they tried to persuade her, the more stubbornly she resisted. Then two of the girls from the top class came along and said, 'Well, you can take part in our production.' A happy Mara rushed off to do exactly what she stubbornly refused to do five minutes ago.

MENTORS

First, something about thermodynamics. Do you remember how gas molecules behave? They fly around in the space they fill until they bump into other molecules. Then, they bounce off and fly off in another direction and bump into another. (Well, it's boring being on your own, after all!) If we squeeze the gas into a tighter space or place it under pressure, the gas heats up. The molecules are tighter together and they bump into each other more frequently. When the collisions are more frequent, the speed at which they dash around increases and the space is more charged with energy. The same thing happens in a space full of people. The home of Kitezh's director, Sergei Khlopenov, is a good example. In one room there is both the computer room and the 'air traffic control centre,' i.e., the focus of the adults' and children's activities, lessons and problem solving. Living in a community is the melting pot of all human interaction.

Here, Nastya Khlopenov, three years old, once said to her mother, 'I love Petya so much.'

'Why, love?' asked Julia.

'He's the only one who talks to me,' said Nastya, looking down.

Nastya had already noticed that the others politely ignore her. The older kids are too busy. In the maelstrom of activity, she's alone. And an innocent remark from eighteen-year-old Petya, 'So, Nastya, how are you?' is like a precious gift.

Earlier, we thought that if the children are in classes with each other for six hours a day that they would have plenty of time to talk to each other, but that is far from the case. We discovered through discussion and asking direct questions that there can be complete indifference between the kids within a class. Phrases like, 'Pass me your ruler', or, 'Stop looking at my answers' cannot be seen as even a rudimentary stage in creating relationships.

Children have to start exchanging more meaningful comments; there has to be communication on a much deeper level than the everyday. We had tried to raise the interaction of the whole group to a higher emotional and intellectual level. It remained for us to strengthen our familiarity with such a higher dialogue by repetition; to reach a stage where we were happy and comfortable with it and, finally, to make this dialogue a daily habit. This is how the new elements of the inner cultural world of the community were created.

The main role of therapeutic work is to give emotionally damaged children the chance to understand and accept their inner world—to reconstruct their past, and their often traumatic early childhood, to understand that they are able to change the direction of their life.

Children have to learn to be open about their own problems during group work and not to hide or deny them. If they cannot overcome this fear, their emotional development will be slowed and they will inevitably lag behind in their intellectual development.

Children must never be left alone with their problems and fears. Some approaches to psychology view the process of talking about one's problems in a group of sympathetic listeners as having a positive effect that can help a person rid himself of his childhood fears. In everyday life, for many people, that group of listeners is the family or a group of like-minded friends. But orphaned children lack those safe surroundings. Creating it is the main task facing the therapeutic community.

Our children know that our volunteers are always available to give them the attention they need. If they have problems with their parents (who may be pushing them too hard to study and work), they can turn to the volunteers, who will listen to what they have to say. They are generally not afraid of revealing their fairy tales and inner world to the volunteers. It is usually small children, newcomers, or those who have not enough social contact in their family who feel the need for extra attention.

Children who are already comfortable in their families pay little attention to the newcomers.

Therapeutic surroundings should pose challenging problems and obstacles and encourage us to overcome our own imperfections, but it must also offer children the space to be alone at times—to tend to their wounds, as it were, and look upon a situation without fear or haste. We all need support from someone with whom we are not afraid to be honest, whom we trust. In Kitezh, we noticed that support is more often found among older peers than among adults.

No book, however interesting; no computer; no parents despite their great effort, can replace the happiness and the challenges of chatting with like-minded peers. The opinions of informal leaders carry more weight in certain situations than those of a teacher or a parent. This observation and the way our older children were growing up and growing wise so quickly led us to introduce a group of mentors amongst the older children.

All systems tend to sink to the level of inertia; that is to say, everybody aims to adopt a more comfortable, a more horizontal position—best of all, in front of the television. People watch TV and react, 'He's an idiot, but she's cool.' There's nothing to think about. You can sit with a beer in your hand and react without analysing what's going on. That's how apathy grows, and life dies a slow death. That's why we think it important to introduce new topics of conversation into our children's environment and get them interested in ideas and ideological conflicts. They should argue passionately and insist on their rightness, sharpening their reason and wits in the search for conclusions. In this way children develop their conversational skills; they can create new identities, satisfy their curiosity and imagination, 'tread down' the world around them, and assert their part in the community.

The Kitezh Community Reaps what it Sows

THE YOUNG ADULTS STEP UP AS MENTORS AND
COMMUNITY LEADERS

It was sometime at the beginning of 2000 that we started to sense quite acutely that we really didn't have enough adults in Kitezh. We were having to depend more and more on collaboration with the children. At first, the older girls started to look after the little ones in the kindergarten and in their families. The older boys proved to be very useful when it came to working on building projects. Several experiments showed us that our boys and girls could be seen as a real reserve when the adults' strength was at an ebb.

Then, following the above logic, we began to turn to the kids for help in one of the most important spheres: teaching school lessons. In any case, we had no other option. The professional teachers in Kitezh could not, even with the best will in the world, manage the basic curriculum with the number of children we had. So each student of the top class was asked to teach one lesson a day (in any subject they were happy with) in one of the younger classes. Our Year Eleven students took up the idea enthusiastically. Teaching was for them a way to assert and increase their authority. At the same time, it increased their own knowledge, allowing them to look at what they had learned in a new way. The saying, 'The third time you explain something you understand it yourself' became very popular.

The experiment had much deeper consequences. The following is an extract from my notes in December 2002:

The older classes have stopped thinking of themselves as 'objects to be taught'. They can look at certain problems in the community from an adult perspective since they have tried on the role of the teacher. The walls have gradually started to disintegrate between the generations. It only took two months, July and August 2002, for the crystallisation to take place in the children's collective. The educational methods introduced by us a few years ago have become a strong cultural element in the community and one of the most important forms of work where adults and children combine their efforts. Last winter, Year Ten had only learned to replace us formally in the younger classes, but now they keep an eye on discipline and every child's mood themselves. They have heart-to-heart conversations with the younger ones, give them advice, instructions and comfort, and apportion them punishment. All this has happened less than nine years after the arrival of the first settlers on the territory on which we have built Kitezh.

Wherever possible, we try to acknowledge the authority of those students who demonstrate outstanding intellectual development and laudable values. We don't make their life easier and we don't accord them extra privileges, as this would arouse envy and lessen their authority among the other children. (I remember how we used to hate the 'teacher's favourite' at school.) But in Kitezh, interaction between adults and children is much more frequent and therefore closer than in other places. The slightest remark from one of the adults can therefore be a great source of encouragement and acknowledgement of someone's value.

In order not to violate Kitezh's vow of honesty and sincerity, I would add that our children are not all ready to accept encouragement or criticism from all of the adults, and not everything that is said by our adults is taken as the last word. In our community we have trust but not blind subordination or fanatical devotion. In all cases, young people must have the right to choose and the chance to discuss things sensibly and openly.

From my diary, December 2002:

The Teachers' Council has asserted that within the framework of the Youth Council and at its meetings, the children are able to draw solid conclusions and make sensible judgments about what happens in the community, to discuss their problems openly, to solve petty conflicts, and to give praise and mete out punishment without adult interference.

The younger ones, seeing that all the older children behave concordantly and support the same principles, try their hardest to do the same. They are not yet able to understand all of our aims, but they take the culture of interaction in Kitezh for granted now and try to be like their older peers.

Gradually, the adults' world view penetrates into the consciousness of the thinking and acting teenager. It is very important that it is not seen as a command or an obligation. When it is, young people automatically switch on their defence mechanisms. When the community puts pressure on children or points out to them an opportunity to grow or gain authority, then they tend to take it.

Ideally, we hope to make colleagues out of our mentors and help others to become leaders as well. When that happens, everyone can become a leader in some way. Among the children, we will have a circle of active, confident people who share our positive world view and whose orientation reflects active collaboration with the adults.

'I've just started to understand you grown-ups better!' This exclamation from the Year Tens has become music to my ears. Having become familiar with the problems of the younger ones, these boys and girls had started to understand their own problems better in relation to their parents and teachers. It is amazing how breakthroughs like this have made life and work easier for all of us. A general understanding of problems emerged and rivalry gave way to mutual support and love. Conversations between adults and children began to be full of understanding and trust. Sometimes it seems that I can physically sense how consciousness has expanded in volume in the older classes. They have suddenly started seeing Kitezh as a whole and are showing interest in what others are going through deep down. They easily consume adult books and argue, not about songs or pop groups, but about theories of understanding and moral laws.

Now, the older children in Kitezh interact according to a common way of thinking. A film prompts wide-ranging discussion and a group attempt to understand it and agree on its essence. Discussion gets more complex with every new experience. The children use phrases and concepts that they have learned in lessons and from the TV. The children's newspaper has helped us create an intellectually rich and full environment for dialogue. Now almost all the schoolchildren in Kitezh have had the chance to express their ideas publicly on questions that interest them and talk about themselves. The editorial team of the paper collects and edits articles and arranges the layout. The children develop a dialogue on contemporary topics and themes. These then become incorporated into their everyday discourse.

Thus we become enriched by our environment and our development flourishes, making our conversations all the more enjoyable and significant. Talking has become great fun, and expanding our intellects is highly valued. To strengthen this process, we encourage all kinds of communal projects or activities and parties involving younger and older kids together. In this way, our values and norms of behaviour are carried over to the younger children.

This is poignantly described in the following poem written by Svetlana, in Year Nine:

I don't have the words to express
Everything that my soul is telling me.
I choked on my tears
When I tried to think without hurrying.
I was so touched and shaken
By the depths of my history,
It made me aim higher within myself
And not see an adult or a child in you.
It's so long that I've been searching for stars.
Now my crying has dug into my chest,
And I don't think it will be easy,
But I know that I'll check what you mean.
You're somewhere; perhaps you're right by me,
But my path doesn't pass by you.
I'll overcome all barriers so I can
Enter the circle as an equal.

16

An Ode to Mentors and Role Play

Some parents are under the illusion that the cleverer children are, the more easily they can deal with their inner problems. We also thought that, but it turned out to be far from a universal truth, if there is any truth in it at all.

This is an extract from a description of Nina, written in 2002:

She is twelve and quite happily reads the books that we give to Year Ten. More importantly, she understands their content and can analyse adult problems from the point of view of an adult. She has an excellent knowledge of history and uses it to analyse things going on around her. She remembers her past and understands the present. Because she understands, she is afraid.

In our 'humanistic and enlightened' social consciousness, there is a myth that talented children in Russia are born into comfortable, professional Moscow families and that they should fill our capital's universities. I would like to shake up this preconception with the story of Nina's life.

Dimitry: Let's think about the beginning of your life. Can you recall your very first memory?

Nina: I was three. I remember my papa leaving. He said goodbye. I can remember the cupboard in the room. He came and picked me up, then put me down and left. It was a final goodbye.

Dimitry: Think back again. How do you know that you were three? Why is this your first memory? What about other things? The smell of the grass? The first time you fell over? Can you remember the first time you hurt yourself? The first time you were really happy?

Nina: I don't really remember.

Dimitry: Are you sure?

Nina: Yes, I'm sure. My father leaving, that's really my first conscious memory.

Dimitry: Can you remember the colours and the smells?

Nina: No, it's just black and white. It's so long ago; I remember it like a scene in a photo.

Dimitry: Is it a painful memory?

Nina: Now it is a bit. I was so young that I didn't really understand what was happening. Now I look back at the time differently. I remember myself in kindergarten and I didn't see any difference between me and the other kids. I didn't know that my mother and I were poor or that it was strange that I didn't have a father. From the three-year-old point of view, I thought it was normal. Even when I lived in the children's home, I didn't see it as a tragedy. At the time, it was more like a fun adventure. [That's the most important thing: Nina didn't know her life was worthy of pity, so in the children's home, she continued to develop confidently, both emotionally and intellectually.]

Dimitry: Is what I've written here fair?

Nina: Yes, to start with. Then I had to start closing up. After the children's home, we kept getting moved from one place to another, and that crushed me. There were some nurses in those places who would really shout whenever I tried to talk to someone. There was one nice psychologist lady. I could talk to her. But another lady came and eavesdropped on our conversation one day. I was eleven then. I was telling the psychologist that my tooth hurt and that nobody would do anything to help me. And the woman who eavesdropped must have thought I was complaining about her, because she started shouting at me, 'You snitch, always complaining!'

Dimitry: What did you learn from that?

Nina: That you should always talk in an office, where there's no one listening. Well, I learned to keep quiet.

Dimitry: Let's go back to your first memories. Tell me what you remember about your mama.

Nina: When I was little everything was fine. I loved going to the *dacha* with my mama. We used to get up at six and walk through Kaluga. The streets would be empty and it would be quiet and cold. We used to take the train, which I loved so much; it was great. When I was five, I asked Mama to make a fire. She stopped digging the potatoes, made a fire for me, and I baked a potato for each of us on the fire. We had loads of potatoes. We even used to make our own starch.

Dimitry: Why did your father leave?

Nina: Mama told me he had gone to another woman. She told me he's got another wife now and children, but my granny said he was an alcoholic too. So I don't know what's true.

Dimitry: Why did your mother start drinking?

Nina: It might have been because my brother died. She drank a bit before that too, but just a bit. She used to go to work and then she'd pick me up from the kindergarten. My brother was twenty. I'm quite a late child. I don't remember where he used to work but I know he used to love taking photos. He used to lock himself in the bathroom and shout, 'Don't turn on the light, I'm developing pictures.' And he used to love fishing. We always used to have fish hanging above the stove to dry out. I was always following Mama around, even when she was drinking; I was like her tail, always following her around. My granny and my neighbours used to tell me things about my mum. They said that she was a bad mother, but I shouted that she was good. I didn't love my granny when I was little. I even wrote a book, when I was little, maybe seven, all about the dogs and cats that I had tried to rescue. The main tragedy that I wrote about was when my granny tried to take the dog away from me that I had brought in from the street.

Then when Mama started beating Granny, I realised that Mama was bad and perhaps that made me grow up a bit. We started to call out the police quite often. A lady police officer came round. She was nice and helped me understand that my mother was wrong to behave that way with us. Then a policeman came again and I recognised him. They sat with Mama and talked to her in the kitchen. I could hear everything, because I stood behind the door. The policeman asked why she drank and tried to reason with her. I think I wanted to cry then.

Dimitry: Did you cry often?

Nina: I did then, yes. I used to cry because I was so confused by the contradictions, I didn't know whether Mama was really bad or good. It used to feel like the house was shaking. She would beat Granny, I would run to the neighbour for help—'Aunty Shura, Mama's hitting Granny again'. Granny often used to say to Mama, 'Think what you're doing.' Mama had a job as a plasterer and she earned quite a lot. She had quite a lot of work on the side. Sometimes she brought home cash. In the year when there was high inflation, we even had a whole million rubles at home. I remember being really proud of it. But then, when she started drinking heavily, we didn't have enough money for food.

Once, she disappeared for three days. I rummaged around in the kitchen and found a chicken leg, already roasted. So I heated it up and tried to make it last all that time. Then Granny came round and when she found out she made a huge fuss and fed me. She was my granny, after all.

Dimitry: Why did it take you so long to decide to move to Kitezh?

Nina: I'm conservative by nature and I wanted just to carry on at school in Kaluga, like I'd started. I was really scared that the headmaster and especially the social worker would try and talk me out of it. I don't have anything against the social worker, but she was such a sneaky little rat that she could have tricked me. She used to ask me such mean questions and I was only twelve.

Dimitry: So you came to Kitezh and discovered to your surprise that it isn't easy to make friends.

Nina: Of course it wasn't easy. I came in Year Eight. There were already two girls, Masha and Katya. They had been together since the first year of school so why should they let this stranger, Nina, into their gang, especially since I was better at most subjects than them. I could see that they didn't want to be friends with me. I wouldn't say I was desperate to be with older people, either. But I wanted somebody to be with. If not with people my age, then it had to be someone older.

Dimitry: It was difficult to make friends with the older kids, too. Did that upset you?

Nina: I don't really remember. I had Victor at home; he always used to fight with me. I was used to the children's home where everyone teases each other, but I couldn't figure out how serious Victor was when he had a go at me. Now, for example, I understand that he's joking, but then I took it all really seriously. I used to get so upset, even to the point of hysterics. I wasn't at all confident. I had been good at school since the first year, though.

Dimitry: Do you remember complaining three years ago, 'Lots of people don't like me, even more than I expected'. You were very sensible in that you could understand what was happening, but you didn't have the maturity to just ignore it and stop yourself from thinking about the past.

The following is from my diary of the Teachers' Council, when Nina was thirteen: 'Nina's friends have not yet started to think about the kinds of problems that bother Nina. They can't share her experience or support her at difficult times. This intensifies her feeling of ostracism and loneliness. It's the eternal problem of "Woe from Wit". Can a person who acutely feels how different she is, really be happy?'

I think being different can be a source of happiness. But we need to grow into that way of thinking; we need to learn to understand it. At Nina's age, the most important thing is feeling that you belong to a group that somehow respects your individuality. Nina, who is very sensitive and intelligent, understands that she doesn't belong to any group. What can she do? In two or three years, if she can develop emotionally as well as intellectually and if her experience of talking to her peers brings her happiness and confidence, then the problem will vanish on its own. Then Nina will discover that she is loved.

Right now, however, it is painful and psychological pain can change the direction of her development, and give rise to an inadequacy complex or serious obstacles to her path into the future. Her strong side is her ability to reason. If there is a way to break through to her inner world, it is probably through her reason. We must help her move away from reflection and concentrate instead on seeking success in new areas.

For talented Nina to develop normally, she needs to get the most out of our developing environment. She is strong and so she needs an environment that is challenging, though not excessively, so it doesn't use up all her strength, and so that she is never far from triumph. She needs self-confirmation and recognition on the part of those around her because it is precisely this vitamin that transforms the inner world and drives a person on to overcome inner obstacles and aim for perfection.

Kitezh

This is an extract from a later conversation:

Dimitry: Now you're fifteen. What motivates you to study now when you don't have the strict pressure that you were used to in an ordinary school?

Nina: Habit, most of all. I have always been very sure about having to study. I've got a very strong sense of obligation.

Dimitry: Where did you get your motivation from when you were little?

Nina: I don't know, probably when I read books about Lenin. I read a lot and something obviously stayed with me. I wanted to be good… And then, school was always about self-confirmation for me. If nobody wanted to be friends with me, then I didn't really have anything else to do except study. Now I think that I should go to the university and keep on studying. I want to set a good example to the younger kids, whom we expect to work hard in their lessons.

Dimitry: What do you think of the first elections to the Youth Council?

Nina: Actually, it was only after that that life got much fuller and interesting for me. The first year here was quite boring. When the elections started, I was interested in what was going to happen next. When I was little, I used to go with Mama when she went to vote, so I knew what was going on. But I couldn't imagine myself as a member of the Council. Then the summer games started… I remember we made a vow to work with our past. We worked with the sentence 'I have put my past in the past'. I was in a group with Olga and Pasha. My mentor was Pasha but I was a bit scared of him. Olga was like a shock absorber and I could open up a bit more with her there. I talked to her recently and she said that I can be quite difficult to talk to. I didn't want to talk about my past. Why should I suddenly want to? Pasha's not my brother or an old

208

friend, but a complete stranger to me, so I didn't understand why I should tell him.

Dimitry: Do you understand now?

Nina: I think so, yes. Now I explain it to Lilya. Your past and your failures and your fears all stop you from living happily. When I remember the past, I turn cold and I feel horrible inside. It was only recently that I learned how to throw away bad things, to forget them. You shouldn't drag even little trifles with you from your past. I feel better since I've learned that.

Dimitry: Do you realise that you are now a completely different person? Do you take any responsibility for your past?

Nina: I'm not sure. Yes, I definitely feel that I'm a different person, but I'm not sure about the responsibility. In the past that was certainly me, too, but I don't really feel guilty in any way about things I did in the past. When I was younger, I used to torture myself over tiny mistakes, but not any more. Now, I see that you can't make any difference to what's in the past. But I can't allow myself to make the same mistakes in the future.

I can't really believe that I'll ever be a member of the Council but now I understand that soon I'll have to be, or at least a mentor. Only a year ago, Olga was helping me, and now I've got rid of most of my inner problems and I'm helping Lilya and Dasha…

I can't believe that I'm going to be the chief editor of the paper after Pasha, now that he's gone to university in Moscow. Of course, I love Pasha but I like the thought that he's not going to be around to kick me as the chief editor. I realised that when they kick me, I still want to work. Last year, he even sacked me from my post. I forgot to put out an issue on time. By the way, after he sacked me, we actually got on better. Until then, I saw Pasha as someone who was always shouting or swearing. Then I realised that you can actually talk to him about all kinds of different things.

Dimitry: What future do you imagine for yourself?

Nina: I can only really think about the very near future. Like tomorrow's the first of September and there's going to be a disco. I don't really look far into the future.

Dimitry: Still, try and imagine, roughly. Strict programmes for the future never work out anyway. Just describe the rough contours.

Nina: University, studying, exams. It's vague but I guess I'm already preparing for it psychologically. By the way, thanks for the idea about the strict programme. I'll remember that as my discovery for today. I want to be able to travel around the world and see other countries. The world is huge. I've never lived in Moscow; life seems to be so different there to Kaluga and Kitezh. Our community really is a special place.

Dimitry: So, would you like to live in Moscow?

Nina: Not for long. I don't know what I'd do there yet. We went to Moscow two years ago. I walked around and thought that I loved the city and that I'd like to live there. But I think I've changed my mind. Now I'm not so bothered about living in a city and life in Kitezh seems more interesting and fulfilling.

There is, however, another kind of 'undercover' leader who prefers to appear weak on the outside. More often than not, they are scared of disappointing themselves and so avoid testing themselves. For this category of leaders (they most often lead the opposition), we also need to create a particular kind of environment. They should be faced with challenges to help them break out.

ALEXEY'S STORY

Alexey came to us in Year Five. He had lived in a children's home for most of his life, where he had made profound discoveries about the art of survival. 'I hate it when someone is rude about my parents!' he says. Yet his parents were alcoholics and violent, which meant that Alexey had to learn to look after himself and avoid being beaten. Alexey's world view allowed him to deal with the challenges of survival successfully for five years: to steal food, avoid contact with adults, and find a place to sleep in the cab of a lorry when his front door was locked.

When Alexey came to Kitezh at the age of ten, he was very reluctant to exchange his world view for a new one. Before his eyes was a new world, but in the depths of his consciousness nothing had changed, and Alexey continued to steal, fight and run away.

His foster parents tried to make him do his homework and his teachers tried to make him respond in class. He would cry and get nervous, which made him smoke more, and where was he going to get cigarettes if he didn't steal them? Neither he nor we could see a way out of this vicious circle.

After he got acclimated to Kitezh and had defined his position within his foster family, Alexey gave a petition to the Teachers' Council, in which he wrote: 'I don't want to live in the X family. If you can't change my parents, please send me back to the children's home where I came from.'

Our attempt to scare him by sending him back for two weeks was not particularly successful. He adapted very quickly back to life in the children's home, regained his authority, and from the look of things, was quite at home. He only returned to Kitezh after we had promised to let him move in with another family. It was then that we realised that only a wilful leader could stand up for himself in this way—which meant that we had to work with him. We just had to stimulate his development and desire to gain some responsibility and to help the other children in some way.

First we had to change his living situation again within the framework of Kitezh. To be honest, there weren't any families with free space, so the Teachers' Council reluctantly decided to pass him over to Vadim, who had just got divorced and was impressively raising his three boys independently in a mixture of good will, trust and freedom. At that time, Vadim was also in charge of the potato farming operation and he had little time to chase after the boys or worry about what they were up to.

Under normal circumstances, handing children over to a single man might seem a crime that no social worker would allow, but in our community the function of parents is a bit different: to provide the security of a home and honest, open conversation. Alexey talked to his mentor every day and he started to feel at home with his new, demanding, but safe circle of friends.

When I asked Alexey to tell me about his plans and dreams for the future, he frowned, scratched his head and eventually said, 'I don't know.'

I said, 'Well, try to imagine, what do you want, who do you want to be, what do you want to do?'

'I don't know.'

For comparison I tried the same game with some of the other youngsters of his age. All but one of them gave the same answer. So then we tried a simple imagination game. 'Close your eyes. Imagine a house that you would like to have. Describe it. How many rooms does it have? What can you see in the rooms? Where are your computer and your guitar? Where are you? Who do you want to be in five years?'

When we were talking about computers, it was easy, but

nobody could really imagine themselves. I admit that this was pretty unexpected. In childhood I loved imagining myself as a grown-up. I used to draw vivid pictures about my imagined life, in which I compensated for all my weaknesses and mistakes. Every day, lying in bed, I would spend hours thinking about how big, strong and clever I was soon going to be. Oh, youthful vanity! How the girls would drop at my feet! (Girls! An eternal worry and a powerful stimulus to growing up!) Alexey was twelve when he stopped saying that he didn't need anything and that he didn't care about anything. He started to care about Varya and he started listening to people's advice about how to be grown up and get her attention. The near future had finally started to be of interest to him. He learned Photoshop so he could make Varya a photo card for her birthday. He took part in the table tennis competition. He even started doing his homework!

All this forced our young hero to redirect his world view towards growing up. One of his first open discussions with adults started with girl questions: 'What should I do so that she notices me? What should I be like?' Over the next year or so, Alexey's trust of others in Kitezh grew immensely and he shook off his former anxiety. Then he could start taking advice when he needed it. All of a sudden, the outer world exerted an influence on his development. This was the start of an utter transformation. The world around him changed. Alexey's friendship with Varya lost its urgency, but, thankfully, his recognition of himself as a leader and a responsible person remained.

A month later, Alexey discovered he was being carried away in the bustling stream of social interaction and that he had neither the will nor the strength to break free from its grip. Now he could see a vision of the future. He started to dream about being big and good-looking, earning lots of money, living in Kitezh, and that everything would be 'cool!'.

In 2000, Alexey's chronically poor progress had been discussed by the Teachers' Council no fewer than ten times. By 2002, he had really started working. In some subjects he was getting Cs, in others As. Sometimes, out of old habit he would test his teachers' nerves by not doing his homework, but mainly his consciousness expanded immeasurably. He had discovered that there were countless interesting and essential things to do besides illicit smoking. The promise of a trip to Moscow or of getting some boxing gloves became sufficient motivation for intellectual effort on his part. Clearly, his desire to become one of the group had prompted his new adult behaviour. It might not be stretching things to say that he even started to enjoy reading.

The most powerful stimulus, besides trips and excursions—for Alexey as well as the rest of the young Kitezhans—became the computer and even the traditional way of passing the time: books. Alexey stopped stealing.

We have to admit that we didn't really provide Alexey with a full and proper family life. He didn't get a mother's affection and his relationship with his foster father, Vadim, was more brotherly than fatherly. Nevertheless, even in these not ideal circumstances, a well-thought-out and consistent approach to parenting allowed Alexey to gain confidence and a valued place in the collective and to start developing intellectually. He still didn't always see it as necessary to observe all the limits and laws of our community, but this also allowed him to make unusual decisions. He is still one of the physically smallest in his class, but in the summer role-playing game he stood out as a leader and one who knew what responsibility meant. Quite unexpectedly, he led his team to victory in the game, which strengthened his resolve and readiness to develop according to a new and positive life programme.

The following article, written by Pasha, our school leader and newspaper founder, gives a clear sense of what the summer game is all about:

The summer has been and gone! This summer saw the creation of the first psychological camp in Kitezh. The aim of the project was to capture us sinners and the kids who came from children's homes in the Kaluga district to stay with us for two weeks and plunge us into a fairy tale that reflects a fantastic, alternative world.

The idea for the camp sprang from the books, *The Lord of the Rings* and *Harry Potter* and the film *Merlin*—namely, the idea of teaching magic in the best academic tradition. All the younger kids in Kitezh and the new arrivals were split into two 'faculties' that were again divided into four levels of difficulty. This formed older and younger classes. The older students, who were trained for two weeks by Merlin, the founder of Kitezh, served as mentors. They were to monitor the psychological state of the students, lead enlightening discussions and teach magic. The classes were to be granted privileges in the form of different magical attributes; for example, Class Four had magic wands that could be used to turn younger students to stone. Each of the classes had magic spells they could utter, like 'freeze', 'be silent', and so on. Those without magic wands could conjure up magic when they earned enough reward points. One spell cost five points, which they could earn only by kissing the magic stone of science or by performing services. (Those cunning Kitezh adults!)

So it was to be a competition between the faculties. This was the source of no small amount of excitement, for children and adults alike. Kitezh was on the very brink of a civil war! Their passions were stirred by their loyalty to their team colours, their especially composed hymns, their emotive speeches and their propaganda! This partisan war almost spun out of control. The fever rose to such a point that even the dining room, supposedly a holy sanctuary, turned out to be nothing of the kind and was divided as fiercely as the whole territory. The two rows of tables at which the faculties sat were separated by a political no-man's land and a wall of adults.

Two buildings—the school and the hostel—were designated as game locations. From the dining room, the two faculties rushed to their respective buildings, which were filled with symbols of 'power fields' in the form of crosses, wooden pyramids and coats of arms. The 'red' camp (the people of fire) had an Egyptian cross as their coat of arms, while the 'blues' (the people of water) chose the snail as their symbol. These coats of arms appeared everywhere, even on the cheeks of the players. Each team created legends about the origin of the world, and developed tactics of partisan warfare in the impassable forest. The children had learned to bow to the will of their leaders and to help each other in difficult moments after more than a week of preparation and training.

And then, the final stage! We were divided into four teams, each with its own route to complete, and its own leader, who was to lead the team to its unknown destination. The journeys were different for each team but they each traversed the forest thicket, which was imbued with all kinds of folklore and mythology. The expeditions were interspersed with 'stations'—places where courage was put to the test.

An hour before midnight, the teams set off on their heroic exploits. Night had devoured everything, with the darkness broken only by the occasional campfire. Among them crept witches, werewolves and vampires. Many of these haunting figures were unknown to us, as they took the form of our guests from good old England or less old America. So, we were dwelling in the twilight land of hobbits and fairies. Amidst all the terror, the teams scurried around, chasing the clock to get to their goal. Who will get there first? Who will get the cake and, more importantly, the glory? The divided territory; the cunning riddles at the campfire stations; strange hands grabbing the bottoms of trousers from the bushes around us; some mad old witch in disguise; confusion; passions running high…

During the game, you can't think logically or consequentially. The bright flames of urgent decisions and quick realisations flash by like tracer bullets in the foggy darkness. But this time, as a mentor, I observed the game from the sidelines, which turned out to be no less involving than playing. The players' passion was infectious, and when you run with the team, you too become prey to the excitement and nervous energy.

In the final battle, there wasn't the customary division into reds and blues. Each team fought for itself, every team member had to go through his trial and prove his worth. And they really proved themselves! In Vanya's team (he was our guest from Sukhinichy orphanage) a witch turned one of their warriors to stone as punishment for a wrong answer. Vanya picked him up and carried him on over his shoulder! On another team, the leader, Anna, broke down, so in the forest, the team chose a new leader, Vova, who led the team to the end. In the last sprint to the finishing line, Vova lost a trainer and ran barefoot across stones and twigs. But he got there and, howling (from excitement and pain in his foot), he celebrated his victory! Alexey, the leader of the victorious team, had been confronted by a dragon and had to choose between giving up on the expedition or sacrificing one of the team members. And he had sacrificed himself! Touched by the selflessness of the team leader, the dragon pitied the team and let them all go free. Alexey and his three warriors got the cake that night and a standing ovation. But it was everybody who got to the end that was a victor.

What to say in conclusion? The game was so emotional that all of Kitezh got carried away by it. Even the mentors sometimes forgot about their educational role and got caught up in the kids' enthusiasm in their struggle for glory. And only Merlin (a.k.a. Dimitry Morozov) could bridle the chaos and put everyone back on to their original quest for enlightenment.

Five of our young visitors to Kitezh were so impressed by what they got up to that they asked to stay with us. Vanya has stayed and he's going to be in Year Nine. Judging by how he led his troops through the forest, we can confidently say that he's going to be a valued new member. Two of his younger brothers are staying, too.

The game has resulted in real changes in the kids' relationships with each other. Mutual respect has emerged on all sides. It's all been about discussing and making decisions together as a group, and we can conclude the experiment has been successful. Let's do it again!

As an historian, I'm fascinated by the cyclical processes in childhood. Without any prompting, the more active members of the Youth Council, who are excited about Kitezh's future and plan to come back, have started to identify and train their successors from among the more active and promising younger children. In the game, by having to lead their teams, the leaders were confronted by situations that required them to develop new qualities and skills, to create new rituals for making decisions within the group, and to agree on certain rules of behaviour. Even individual agreements and contracts were settled. It might seem to some like a junior version of democracy, but I genuinely think that within Kitezh, people have to learn to agree on everything. Gradually, their own experiences convince our children of this truth.

A system based on a model of an objective world has proven

to be capable of fostering self-development. But it has to be an integrated system. It's not enough simply to explain the rules of the game to children; any motivation will only remain in place for a limited period of time. You need an external motivation that allows the participants to step back from their inner uncertainty and help put the child in a positive state of mind. When these have become consolidated, you can expect longer spans of concentration on achieving ambitions. But in all cases, let's not forget that Pavlov proved that basic reflexes arise not from instantaneous moments of revelation but through frequent repetition.

But so as not to arouse your suspicion about the truthfulness of what you're reading, we should note that our young mentors don't always get what they want. Pasha and Olga came to see me one evening for tea, themselves in a boil.

'We don't know what to do about Phillip,' Olga said, with tears welling up. 'We've been talking about it all week at the Council. He's not allowed to use the computer or to go to the discos but he still doesn't do his homework and behaves like an idiot.'

'I'll hit him soon,' added Pasha, despondently.

I enquired further. 'Do you remember what has happened to this unhappy boy? Before Kitezh, all he had seen was drunk and violent parents and neighbours who were no less drunk. His faculties of reason are not yet fully developed and the world is like a big, heavy sledge hammer that comes down on his head without rhyme or reason.'

'But we don't touch him!' exclaimed Olga, hurt. 'We even wrote a contract with him where he promised he would do his homework and be cooperative.'

'I expect he forgot about the contract an hour after signing it, otherwise he would have stuck to it,' I replied. 'Don't forget, he doesn't see the world in the same way you do. He's working on it—he's gradually starting to comprehend the motives of those around him—but this is a slow process that could take years, and you can't change that. Think about yourself, Pasha, three years ago. You didn't understand everything that was going on, either, but your parents didn't hit each other on the head with saucepans and you weren't terrified of the adults around you.'

'So, are you saying we shouldn't punish him?'

'Punish him, make him do his homework and make him think, but remember, you probably won't see any results for about two years. So keep your nerves in one piece. And just so you can relax, remember that as well as Phillip there's Zhenya in the same class and he's standing up for his rights. We've got lots more kids like him ahead of us.'

The happy end to this story was that Olga and Pasha carried on trying to get through to Phillip. And they still are.

17

The Essence of the Kitezh Therapeutic Approach

CULTIVATING THE FIELD OF THE CONSCIOUSNESS
(OR THE COMMUNITY CIRCLE)

Behaviour patterns learned in early childhood are resilient but they can be erased—or rather, replaced by new patterns. We need only remember that basic reflexes are not learned overnight, nor are they acquired by the repetition of instructions, exhortations or punishments. They arise from personal, emotional experiences. That is the essence of Kitezh's educational and parental approach. We see it as entirely useless to tell children repeatedly what they should be like. A child is by nature a sovereign personality, instinctively striving to draw his own conclusions and make her own decisions. If we want to change the examples of behaviour that are imprinted in the archives of their consciousness, we then have to present them with many life situations in which they can independently become convinced of the fallacy of these prior examples. The educational process in this case differs from everyday life only in that we try to ensure that such situations occur frequently and repetitiously, in high concentrations over short periods. In this way, recognition is achieved sooner.

Realisation is closely linked with another state of mind: the expanding of one's consciousness. Expanding the consciousness is moving into a position that allows one to see everything in its true scale. (Unfortunately, the phrase has been sullied by intellectual drug users who use psychedelic drugs to experiment with their own consciousness. In our view, the use of drugs in any kind of therapeutic work is unnatural and counterproductive.)

To convey what we mean by expanding consciousness, let's go back to *War and Peace* and Prince Andrei Bolkonsky, who is lying wounded on the battlefield at Austerlitz. Until this moment he has been dreaming of personal glory, and in his imagination, he has pitted himself against no less a man than Napoleon. The war is raging (though not quite as he had imagined), the Russians are suffering great losses, all around him are bodies; but the Prince isn't interested in trifles. His consciousness is focused on his higher goal, his quest for glory. Everything around him, even fear of his own death, is pushed to the background. Perhaps half way to his glory, an explosion knocks him to the ground and his inner world is shaken out of place. Now, he is given the opportunity to lie on his back motionless, and from this new perspective he sees something he'd never really noticed before: the sky.

The sensation of proximity to death and therefore to God clears his consciousness of such trifling thoughts as Napoleon and personal glory. Instantly, his inner programme is reset as his life values are assessed in a flash before his eyes. He survives and learns to notice the variety in natural phenomena. His hardened character softens and a new emotional force awakens in him. The therapeutic interference of the cannonball opens our hero's world to love, new feats of daring and new disappointments, to everything that we would call a full and meaningful life.

But consciousness-expanding experiences alone don't add up to much. They only give one the chance to look at things a bit differently and lift inner blockages. I have worked with children for whom a consciousness-expanding experience hasn't led to self-actualisation but has tempted them to enter a cult.

Frightened by their recognition of the limitlessness of the world and the endlessness of possibility, they were tempted to submit to a sect of fanatics and to hand themselves over to the first person with a clear and certain agenda and persuasive convictions. What happened was something like an imprint. The first one to say, 'I know how to protect you from the world' was taken on as a master who could bend and subject the consciousness of this unconfident person to his own will. As with any medication or treatment, work on realisation and expanding consciousness is best done with the participation of professionals and not alone.

The second component of the educational process is to help children understand the situation they are in. The conclusions a child makes are as good for him as medicine is for a sick man. In the process of open and honest discussion (in psychological terms, 'therapeutic dialogue'), a mentor can help a child see his situation more broadly and prompt him to draw conclusions from it. In that way, the discovery will be the child's own. He will remember it because he will associate it in his consciousness with the happy feeling of triumph. Discoveries should become a constant part of life, for the frequency of feelings of triumph and satisfaction confirms the new pattern of behaviour.

By talking about things that are happening currently, children learn to exert some influence on events and they get used to seeing themselves as responsible for what goes on in their lives. This, however, is only one side of the coin. While one person in a group is talking about his problems, successes or discoveries, the others can try out his evaluation of himself on themselves. They can compare that evaluation with the spontaneous reaction of the group to certain words or actions. Without any external pressure, there is a real lesson going on whereby children can try on other people's identities and models of behaviour. And all of this takes place without the worry of direct criticism from parents or adults in general. This is a natural path inherent in human nature. It is based on fundamental qualities that surface in earliest childhood. Because of it, children can proceed along the path relatively quickly.

A MEETING WHERE NO ONE FALLS ASLEEP

I have sat through many meetings. There have been interesting ones, but most of them I remember as a painful waste of time. The children's meetings in Kitezh are not this kind of meeting. Quite the contrary: they are a most interesting way to spend time, both for children and adults. Most importantly, they are the safest way to make life-changing discoveries and expand consciousness.

Why does a balloon expand? As the pressure from within increases, it exerts a pressure outwards and as the rubber stretches, the balloon can grow. A child is full of discoveries; he is bursting with new impressions that he can't wait to share. (This means the pressure from within is mounting.) The next condition is elasticity, pliability, and flexibility of the mind or consciousness, already achieved through safe and open discussion with a mentor. An environment that has been relieved of tension—that is to say, a safe environment—is all that is needed so that children will wait to hear your story. You will be listened to without judgment and definitely be given sympathy and support. That is the formula for our therapeutic meetings that we introduced into the community with the help of our British friend, David Dean, although we have had to adapt a lot of his ideas to accommodate our national and local idiosyncrasies.

The older children sit with the younger ones and encourage them to express their opinions and relate to what is being discussed seriously. The younger ones are not scared of being 'picked on' by older peers because that doesn't happen in Kitezh.

A lot of the success of the meeting depends on the person leading it. He needs to sense very subtly the mood and needs of every child who speaks. Some need praise; others need nudging when faced with a challenge. For the first six months I led the meetings, but then the members of the Youth Council gradually learned the art. I admit it didn't all run smoothly from the start.

Petya: Zhenya, tell us how you have put the past behind you. [Zhenya says nothing and lowers his head.]

Petya: Just say something. We've been waiting for you all week. When it's other people's turn to talk, you're chatty enough, and now you're silent. [Zhenya still says nothing and keeps his head down.]

At this moment I was called out of the room, and when I got back, Petya had kicked open the door and was dragging out Zhenya, kicking and screaming. A second later and Zhenya went flying from the porch and into the snow. Petya, in defiance of all norms of therapeutic procedure, wiped his hands with satisfaction and shouted: 'And don't come back until you're ready to open up to your friends!'

My first thought was, 'Oh my God, what have I done? How could I leave this therapeutic work to such an immature boy like Petya?' My second thought was, 'Well, Zhenya has had a taste of real life again where no one has limitless patience and endurance'. You can imagine my surprise when, at the next meeting, Zhenya chirped up and spoke. He sat there with a big smile on his face as though nothing had happened previously, and talked openly about his thoughts and feelings in the course of the day. Petya's extreme course of action had been a success.

Excerpts from my diary of 2003:

14 January. Soon after the end of the school holidays we had a psychological game, 'Creators of the World'. The children were

given a set of laws and moral norms that they were to observe over the course of the day. We called this 'the vow'. At the general meeting, a mentor was chosen by general consent from the older classes for each of the younger children. The mentors were obliged to talk to their pupils every day about their psychological problems and to help them observe the laws.

In the evening at the general meeting, the mentors heard everyone speak. This is the dialogue of one of the meetings that Olga chaired as a member of the Youth Council:

Olga: So, kids, tell us: what's been good today? What discoveries have you made? Who did you smile at? What made you laugh?

Masha (thirteen years old and smiling sweetly as if to say I'm only little, don't touch me!): Nothing special. [As if to say, You can go on now, ask someone else.]

Oleg [fourteen, giving out a confident air, in a deep voice]: Everything's fine. (He doesn't yet realise what we want from him.)

Olga: What did you learn today, what did you discover? Who did something brave? Or realised something about themselves or about the world around them? Larissa, why so quiet?

Larisa [fourteen, with a shaky voice and lowered eyes]: Er… I don't know.

Nastya: My day was fine. I went for a walk with Katya. I liked it.

Eva has a distant, dreamy look in her eyes and Phillip's expression seems to be directed within as though what's going on around him hasn't touched him yet. Everyone seems to be paying attention, but there isn't any kind of common sphere of understanding. We have to find a focus of common interest that will hold their attention.

Olga: OK, enough of this rubbish. Is that really a realisation? Try to remember something genuinely new that you managed to understand; something that made you go 'wow!' or that made you cry.

Phillip: I...I liked drawing today... and I quite liked doing my homework. [Is this reply the result of an inner discovery? Doesn't seem like it, but it's still great that Phillip has taken it upon himself to share his experience. Doing homework means 'gaining face' in the group. On the other hand, when I was at school, it was fashionable to outdo one another in our disdain for our homework. It was a matter of dignity that even after you had stayed up all night struggling over your work, when you went into the classroom you told the others, 'I haven't done anything.']

Phillip's task had been to attract the group's attention to his modest person and he had done it in the most natural way for him. There will be a time when he feels confident of the safety of the situation and he will be able to drop the reins in public and actually look inside himself.

Masha: I woke up, washed, went to morning exercises, and then went to school...

Olga: Stop! Masha, this is everyday stuff. We all know your timetable but we want to know about your experiences and feelings.

Masha: I found out that Tanya is coming to stay [Tanya is a student from Tula who comes to teach chemistry] and I was really happy. I realised that I love Tanya.

Vasya (thirteen): Today I did some carving and I made a really nice ornament. It used to take me four hours to make something like that but now I can do it in an hour.

Olga: How did that make you feel?

Vasya: Proud and pleased with myself.

Sveta: Today I talked to my mentor, Olga, and I was really happy afterwards. I had Russian with Larissa and I suddenly understood the exercise. I realised it wasn't so scary after all!

Vladislav: Today I made up with Vasya and we had a good chat (he blushes). I think we're going to be friends again. Damn, I don't know how to say what I felt. I invited him round this evening for supper. [Everyone's really pleased and applauds.]

Olga: Vlad, you see how important it is to everyone that you get on with Vasya.

Alex: Everyone's ecstatic!

Vladislav: Yeah, I know. I'm happy too.

Olga: Vasya, what about you, why didn't you mention it? Didn't you notice your conversation with Vladislav or did it not seem like a new thing for you?

Vasya: Yeah, I noticed it [laughs, embarrassed], and I was really happy. We're friends now. And I'm going to go round for supper.

That's how the tradition of the therapeutic meeting started in Kitezh. The term sounds a bit stiff, but what we're really talking about is a safe circle of friends where the youngsters can throw off their shells and feel themselves a part of an invigorating stream of changes. In the 70s and 80s, during the 'thaw' in Russia, we used to love sitting with friends in the kitchen with a bottle of vodka and discuss life, the universe, and everything. The difference in the 'therapeutic meeting' is that a professional, who doesn't even charge a fee for creating a friendly atmosphere, leads it and there's no vodka involved.

In an ideal therapeutic community, all adults should understand child psychology and control their own feelings to such an extent that their presence at the meetings wouldn't make any difference to the kids. But despite the apparent simplicity of this task, not all adults are able to approach their participation professionally and without special preparation to get into the right frame of mind. When we started the meetings, a few adults were present. We agreed in advance that the adults would resist expressing their feelings, making judgments, or taking control of the discussion.

Now that the tradition is established, the children might not even notice the presence of any adults. If there is a question of general interest being discussed at the meeting, then everyone will go along. An active sphere of trust is created and even the children with the worst complexes find it hard not to give in to its positive influence. We have seen a new kind of competition emerge: the children's determination to prove how grown-up they are by speaking and being heard.

We have found that certain questions give rise to particularly heated reactions—questions like, 'Who's controlling whom?' 'How is that fair?' and 'How do you get people to do what you want them to?' In these situations particularly (although it applies generally as well), the role of the leader is of primary importance.

Children who are busy with the tricky business of growing up need a world view that is based on clearly defined moral criteria, that is integral and attractive in its strength and beauty. The kids will grow up, grow strong, and then they'll choose for themselves which of their childhood beliefs they will retain and which they'll put behind them. Just let them grow up first! Don't rob them of their inner connection with society and country or with a feeling of having a higher task in life.

The most important thing is that children learn to see the inner connection between their life choices and the common good and to understand the clear connection between people's actions and their positive or damaging results. In the meetings we often discuss what we can do with people who disturb the peace or how we can reconcile conflicts. We can't get by with encouragement and praise alone. We have, however, replaced the word 'punishment' with 'compensation', which sounds less harsh and is also more constructive. The children come to see the necessity of paying compensation for every offence against the community and they are not ashamed of the penalty imposed on them.

These meetings, like nothing else, help the children develop: to make sense of their emotions; compare their self-evaluation with the evaluations of others; and become confident that the world around them is familiar and controllable. By opening up at the meetings, the children go through a process of internal restructuring every time they experience an insight, much like a butterfly that has completed its metamorphosis and escapes from its cocoon. But like that fragile young butterfly, a child is very vulnerable at these moments of insight.

During moments of emotional upsurge, doubt, grief or regression, a child desperately needs the support of a group of people who are important to him. This support must be active so that the child is able to perceive it, but not so strong that it disrupts the process.

A child is immersed in varying challenges, emotional contacts, and intellectual stimuli. Some might question whether we can call this environment safe. For those who are used to it, yes, we can. For others, it can be extremely demanding. It is a bubbling cauldron of challenges. But we know that sharing experiences and discoveries holds the key to happiness. It provides a feeling of unity with like-minded people. It is the transformation of a small personality into a creator.

Thirteen-year-old Sasha brought me a crumpled piece of paper on which he had written his first realisation. 'Our mood depends on us, but we also depend on our mood. Our mood changes the way we see the world, but we can also change the mood we're in. Therefore, we can create our own world!'

This was probably the first time in his life that Sasha had realised that he controls his fate. Believe me when I say that he was radiating happiness and inspiration, as if he was a student in a Zen

Buddhist monastery who had solved some ancient riddle. The difference was that Sasha himself had chosen his own seemingly unsolvable paradox to unravel. And the solution was not some abstraction in the back of his consciousness but something practical that changed his relationship to the world and his place in it.

A realisation is a discovery that grips you completely, that bowls you over with its novelty, that makes your heart beat faster. It broadens your picture of the world, helps you adapt your point of view painlessly, and, most importantly, it stimulates activity.

Here is what transpired at one such meeting:

Boris (seventeen): Every day there's something new. Like today, when I read *King Rat*. My mind is still full of this book. It's set in a prisoner-of-war camp where there are American and British soldiers. One of them, an American, tells everyone how rich he had been and how he had everything. That he lived like a king and everyone looked up to him. Then, the war ends and they're released. And suddenly, all their relationships change. He is an ordinary soldier after all, and the status he had acquired in the camp means nothing in the real world. It can happen in real life— that you could just lose everything in one fell swoop. It was quite a scary realisation.

Ivan (nine): This morning I saw the snow and it was so quiet. [That morning in February was magnificent. Everything was covered in white, fluffy snow and the freezing air was brisk. All the adults who went out for morning exercises were transfixed by the utter silence, the otherworldly tranquillity that vanishes as soon as the snow starts to melt. The children don't usually notice such things, as they are more preoccupied with the world of relationships than with the world of nature.]

Misha (thirteen): Today I was responsible for delivering logs, but Nikita and Sergey stopped work early to play on the computer.

Dimitry: What did you learn from that?

Misha: If you don't keep an eye on people, they take off!

Maxim (seventeen) puts up his hand: Today I saw the forest with new eyes. Everything around us seemed different. I saw every tree individually. It's right next to us, but what do we know about it? There are forces there. The trees are alive; there are all kinds of creatures eating each other, some of them are asleep under the snow, hibernating till spring. The birds are fighting to survive. And when I felt all of that power, it sent a shiver down me. It's too big to think about; you can't fit it all in your brain.

Natasha (twelve): I enjoyed doing my homework today. At first I didn't want to do it, but then I made myself do it, and it was fine.

Vladislav (twelve): Perhaps it's not really a discovery, but today I thought that if you do somebody a good turn, then it returns to you. I liked that. [Last year he stopped stealing. This year he's stopped swearing. Now he's in love and is trying to study.]

After writing all that, I read it through and thought how banal this might seem to a reader. We have all read this kind of thing a hundred times, but how often have we been driven to action by knowing this truth? Our knowledge rarely becomes a basis for action; our discoveries don't often compel us to change our world view. At that moment Vladislav realised the importance of good for the first time. This was a personal achievement that brought him the happiness of victory. He blushed from embarrassment, but his eyes sparkled with pleasure at his realisation. I know with certainty that something of it will remain in him, like a revelation, and that means that next time he's faced with a choice he'll find it easier to choose the good option.

Discussions about the secrets of the soul and the joy of realisation become so much more successful and consequential the older and more intellectually developed we become. Children who have grown up in Kitezh talk about such topics much more freely than do their peers in other places. They are open with their friends and 'their' grown-ups, discussing inner personal problems, pointing out mistakes, and finding ways out of tricky situations together. We aren't sure that our approach can be justified in all cases, but within Kitezh, it has gradually become an element of our culture.

Allow me to quote a few more remarks by our children at their meetings. This will give you more of an idea of the great range of topics that are discussed and the profundity of the discussion they are exposed to.

Olga: I was glad when Ksenya told me about her problems. I trust her too. I thought that the more we talk, the more we will grow confident in each other. That's what the community is.

Vera: I was annoyed with Eva. I asked her to mop the floor in the dining room and she said, 'I'm not your servant.'

Dimitry: Why? What are you then, Eva—an academic? You are a servant. You serve the community—all of us—and we serve you. What else can you do for us except clean the floor and jobs like that? So you mop the floor, knowing that you're doing it for the community. Have you forgotten what we said in our vow, 'I'll give only love and support to those around me?' What do you give Vera when you refuse to do what she asks you?

Eva: I understand. [Not very confidently] Vera, I'm sorry. Forgive me, please; I won't be like that again.

Alexei (fifteen): I don't think this is a realisation. It's just something that made me happy. I couldn't take any more physics earlier, so I started reading *The Master and Margarita*. I suddenly felt like I was living inside the book, like I had just fallen into that world. I still feel like it's living inside me. It wasn't like I was reading words. I don't know, it was like living a second life. I shut the book, but it carried on in me. Then I started thinking about the future. I tried to imagine it in different ways. I picked out one of us and started to think what it would be like without him. First I picked Dima. I looked and thought, no way, we would have nothing without him, so I put him back. Then I realised: there's no one in this community we could get by without.

Masha (twelve): Today was the first day I enjoyed morning exercises. I noticed the sun as it was rising. Valya smiled at me and I smiled back. I felt really happy then.

Vera (thirteen): I had an argument with Eva. She said something nasty, but then I thought, 'OK, I'll apologise first.' Maybe then she'll realise sooner. So I went and said I was sorry. She was really happy. But I didn't want to dance after that. It kind of ruined my mood. I sat by myself at the side and started to sulk. Then I tried to get out of that mood. I remembered that yesterday had been such a gloomy day, but that just above the house there was a patch of blue sky and golden light squeezing through that gap down to the ground. I felt better then. I calmed down and then went to dance practice.

Misha: Yeah, I saw that she really managed her feelings well. [Spontaneous applause!]

Alex: I was annoyed with Oleg today. He doesn't like having to try very hard. When we're working, he's always sitting around on his bum. [everyone laughs]

Oleg: I'm getting better. The other day I carried all that coal for Tamara. Usually when Alexei makes me work, I only take half a bucket but then I thought about the vow, 'I'll learn to work and be patient', and I took a whole bucket. I wasn't messing around. I even felt better about it too.

Dimitry: Yesterday you were cheeky to Tamara. Have you apologised?

Oleg: No. I was too embarrassed.

Valya: What kind of realisation was that, then, if you didn't feel like doing anything afterwards?

Dimitry: You don't like making an effort. That's precisely what Alex said.

Oleg: I only realised just now that what I did was so bad.

Alexandra [sarcastically]: Wow, words of wisdom from Alex! [everyone laughs]

Sveta: Today I started learning to sing. The English girl, Janet, helped me find my voice. Today for the first time I felt the sound I could make. It was huge! It was like I could feel it vibrating. Now I want to be an actress! [Sadly, a week later she'd tired of her new hobby and had given it up.]

Valya (thirteen): I had a moment when I shook myself out of being lazy. We had a test and I really couldn't be bothered to do it. Then I remembered the line from our vow, 'I won't give in to laziness', and I shook myself out of it. It was quite easy. I said to the other girls, 'Don't be lazy, wake up!' Everyone smiled and we started working.

Zhenya: I was a team leader for a whole month this summer and I realised that kids can't always do what they're told. For a week they were all fantastic; the team was united and everyone paid attention. Then, suddenly, like a deflated balloon, it was like they all couldn't care less.

Dimitry: What was your discovery?

Zhenya: Just that it's normal—probably a law of nature. People are either full of energy and strength or they are deflated and weak and indifferent. Even adults. You just have to be patient and bring them back to their senses. [A year before, people would have said that Zhenya only shouted and behaved hysterically. But in 2003, Zhenya, Dima and Pasha assumed complete responsibility for summer camp.]

Vera: I was made responsible for organising the work today and the girls listened at first. But then Sveta sent for me and Eva started messing around and refused to do the jobs in the kitchen. I got really annoyed and started to tell her off. I was right to say it but everyone got annoyed with me and no one would do what I asked. So then I was really upset and just left. Now I realise that I was wrong. Everyone including me reacted to the tone more than to the words. Now I'm ready to be in charge again another day, but first I want to apologise.

Alex: Bravo! Applause! [everyone claps]

Pasha: After four days of holiday I suddenly realised that I get bored if I've got nothing to do. Until now, the whole day has been timetabled and really full. You always have to run somewhere, do something, organise something. But during the holiday no one's telling you what to do. And suddenly all the kids have got sour faces and nobody wants to do anything. I thought, what's it going to be like when we're grown up? Nobody chases you to do stuff then, so will I just become really apathetic?

Dimitry: Most do become apathetic. Very few people can force themselves to set goals, to plan their day. Most prefer to live by the rules. When there's no thunder, they don't pray. You have to pull yourself along by your own hair because it is from doing things—making an effort and overcoming obstacles—that you derive your energy. I'll give you a riddle to solve. I've just thought it up. A mentor comes up to Morozov and says, 'Dima, I've figured out everything about Kitezh. We're here to love and to develop our students! Yes?' 'No!' says Morozov.

[They think about the riddle for less than a minute.]

Alex: The mentor's conclusion was too obvious. He only told you that to get praise.

Pasha: He's self-satisfied and not trying to develop. He

thinks up something and then tries to make Dima do the work, as if saying, 'I blurted out something, let the teacher think up how I'm right and how I'm wrong.'

Olga: If Dima said yes, then we wouldn't think or talk about it any more. The mentor is blissfully delighted with himself, so he'll stop growing. But life's a million times more complicated and can't be reduced to just a couple of words. The question is how to love and how to develop.

I think to myself: This is true bliss for me. Our mentors have almost learned to think independently.

18

Heaven on Earth?

When we spoke at the Second Stockholm conference on Children and Residential Care in 2003, our speech aroused, if not criticism, then certainly doubts, yet, all the delegates from five continents agreed that Russia should close its children's homes and place the children in families. They seemed to think we were recommending the establishment of some large, non-governmental institution as a substitute. They hadn't understood that what we were really advocating was an alliance of independent families.

The main concern voiced by many is that after the 'artificial' environment of Kitezh, children will find it hard to adapt to the outside world. There is also the question of whether the children maintain what they have learned when they return to their villages and their real families. An eighteen-year-old who leaves a children's home and goes back under his parents' roof will almost certainly repeat their tragic mistakes. He will have to 'adapt' to drunken relatives who won't accept him into their circle if he doesn't share their behaviour and view points. Young men and women are too young and naïve at that age to return to that endless drunkenness and moral degradation, to the hopelessness, poverty and lack of human dignity, and assert themselves.

In the meantime, Russia still has its system of registration, which is no different from, or more liberal than, under the Soviet system. The law's intention is to ensure that children who become detached from their family still retain the legal right to at least some space in the family household, otherwise they wouldn't have anywhere to go and would be out on the streets. Registration, however, draws them back into the environment from which social services had initially rescued them. Registration becomes not social security but a chain that locks young people to their nightmarish past. Only the strongest of wills can endure returning to such an environment. Of course, in a society based on higher culture and the observance of morals and democratic laws, such questions wouldn't arise. Let's remember the stories of Petya, Anna and Phillip. What would be waiting for them 'back home'?

That's why we say that a child who leaves Kitezh should not have to adapt to his 'native environment'. Instead, he should try to change it to fit his new ideals and goals.

In Kitezh we tell our older children, 'Adapt to the world according to your ideals. Change the world; don't let the deadly nightshade overwhelm your determination. Lift up those who haven't fallen asleep yet, who haven't lost the passion for life.'

In the process of gaining identity, a young person must sometimes turn away from those who were his original inspiration and support. He might not only turn away; sometimes he will need to dissociate himself from his former friends and family members and even refuse all contact in order to build his own personality and independence. We should celebrate the fact that under our guardianship an independent being has emerged and that a person who once depended on us— even if only on our faith in him—has become free.

In order to believe in others, we have to believe in ourselves, courageously and creatively. We must believe that in the depths within us something inconceivably great can grow. We can but grant a child freedom, allow him to be himself, and become a full member of society, with all of its rights and responsibilities and be able to make his own contribution in a personal and not proscribed way.

Sometimes I find it hard to know if we really can talk about personal therapeutic work in a community such as ours. Which of our methods can we call fundamental? Which are the most appropriate? Which should be placed on the back burner? I know for a fact that the next Kitezh will not be the same as this one. It will be built by our children following their own will and dreams. When, in the bright future, there won't be any orphans in Russia, the Kitezh way of life will still remain in those settlements where people live according to their conscience and in harmony with nature and society.

VANYA

It was one o'clock in the morning. Outside, the elements raged. I was writing this book, and my foster son Vanya was in his room studying for his university entrance exam. He had six months to go before finishing school and he was already working himself to the bone in his preparations. From time to time he had made it clear that he was not afraid to join the army if he was called up. I remember that night now as an epiphany—one that would have a profound effect on all of us. He rarely shared his innermost thoughts and feelings, but that night he began to talk about what had been going on with him over the past few months. We sat drinking tea and the conversation became involved and spiritual.

'I can't sleep at night. I'm literally torn apart by questions, mostly about my reasons for living. It's as though my body is on the bed but I am flying. I wonder about how to serve my time here in a better way. Before, I was under the illusion that if I made less effort, I would live longer. Now I know that that was a mistake; you have to push yourself hard. In that way I could do OK in this test on earth. And so I started to work like a madman. This is the third night in a row.'

'So, you've stopped feeling sorry for yourself?'

'I understood that you shouldn't be afraid of letting go of the small things in order to reach the bigger ones.'

'Aren't you sad that you lost so many years? We were urging you to study.'

'Don't be offended, Dima. I think that everyone grows up at their own pace. Even when you tell us exactly how it is, most people won't listen.'

The exact same words were in the book: everyone acts according to what they can see and understand. It was a victory! I almost wept at that moment.

It was no longer important whether he got into the university the first time around or whether he would sincerely thank us at some point for his upbringing and education. We had achieved one of therapy's principal aims: we had given him the ability to create a life programme independently and of sufficient strength to be unafraid of meeting challenges and of taking advantage of all the possibilities the wide world offers.

This wider world now belongs to him.

Afterword

Kitezh is a place of happiness and joyful refuge for Russian children who have been abandoned or orphaned. Kitezh is an exciting place, in stark contrast to the normally depressing conditions for such children in Russia. The Kitezh approach to fostering and educating children in a therapeutic community environment has already proven to be a real alternative to the Russian state system of orphanages and childcare institutions.

Family, community, country—these are steps to knowledge of the world. At Kitezh a child takes those steps side by side with his parents and teachers, deriving support and inspiration from everyone. Kitezhans raise their children with an awareness of beauty in their natural environment and beauty within themselves.

Our long-term plan is to increase the population in Kitezh to one hundred, of which sixty are children, and to create an environment with all the customary amenities of a village. We are building Orion, our second children's village based on the Kitezh model, two hundred kilometres away. Our hope is to build many children's villages in different parts of Russia that will form a network of Kitezh villages for orphaned children. Therapeutic communities cannot be built according to a plan; they must grow organically through our desire to share our attitude to children and our way of life. We believe that raising children and educating them is closer to art than to any kind of profession. Like the way of self-realisation, it must grow though people's consciousness

We have built two villages and given homes to over sixty children during the first fifteen years. This is, in itself, an impressive achievement. Nevertheless, there are one million orphans in Russia—one million children for whom the government can see no other alternative than to place them in institutionalised orphanages. The majority of these children will never fulfill their potential. Statistics from the Russian Ministry of Education indicate that after leaving an orphanage, fifty per cent fall into the high-risk category. Forty per cent of these children commit crimes, including prostitution. Forty per cent are homeless and unemployed. Ten per cent commit suicide within three years of leaving the orphanage. Only four per cent enter higher education.

We believe we have found an alternative. Our adult children are studying at universities and colleges, creating their own families, finding jobs and meaningful careers. Our example must be expanded in order to change the attitude of those who are in charge of policy. Some of our older children wish to become teachers and pass down the experiences they have received here. Perhaps a few of them will find the courage to build their own therapeutic communities based on their first-hand knowledge and understanding. Professionals in the field of childcare have started to show interest in our therapeutic work with children. Foster parents come to us for advice. Local and national government is beginning to take note of our work. With a lot of help and support, we may be able to make a considerable impact on the current situation in our country.

Dimitry Morozov

Dimitry Morozov received a Doctorate from Moscow State University's Institute of the Countries of Asia and Africa in 1982. Having spent a year in India, and influenced by the philosophy of Nicholas Roerich, he took a prestigious job as a presenter on the Russian national *Radio Mayak*. During *perestroika*, when everything became possible, his decision to leave Moscow and retreat to the countryside to build his dream community for foster families and orphans was outrageous to all his colleagues. Fifteen years later, he is the driving force behind two flourishing community villages for children, with plans to create many more. In 2005 he received an Order of Honour, a civil award of the Russian Federation. In 2008, he was appointed to the Inter-Agency Working Group of the Committee for Family, Women's and Children's Affairs in the Russian State Duma. There is a hope that Dimitry's experience of work at Kitezh and his views on education will help the Committee to take a broader view of issues of children's and family problems. He is the author of several books published in Russia, including *Twice Born*, a visionary novel, *Kitezh Community: a Guide for Foster Families* and *Raising Children for a New Generation*. This is his first book to be published in English.

Ecologia Youth Trust

Ecologia Youth Trust, a small charity based at Findhorn in Scotland, has worked closely with the Kitezh Children's Community since it began in 1992 to support its growth and development. Ecologia Youth Trust receives donations on behalf of Kitezh Children's Community, and has raised funds to build houses for foster families, and provided training and expertise in therapeutic education, play and art therapy by some of the finest, most well-respected childcare professionals in Britain. Kitezh runs a popular volunteers programme, organised by Ecologia Youth Trust. A grant from the UK Big Lottery Fund enabled publication of this first edition of *Kitezh: a community approach to raising children in Russia* for which we are all extremely grateful.

For more information please contact

ECOLOGIA YOUTH TRUST
THE PARK
FORRES
MORAY, SCOTLAND
IV36 3TD

info@ecologia.org.uk
www.ecologia.org.uk

KITEZH CHILDREN'S COMMUNITY
KALUZHSKAYA OBLAST,
BARYATINO RAYON,
249650 RUSSIA

kitezh@kaluga.ru
www.kitezh.org

Supported by